SIMPLE CAKE

SIMPLE CAKE

All you need to keep your friends and family in cake

10 cakes, 15 toppings, 30 cake-worthy moments

Odette Williams

Photography by Nicole Franzen

TEN SPEED PRESS
California | New York

For Nana, Nick, Dixie, Matilda, Opal, and Ned

Contents

Cake loves . . .

A house full of comings and goings

Kindness

Meltdowns of epic proportions

A chilled glass of sparkling Moscato d'Asti

An old linen tablecloth

Wet swimmers

Belly laughs

One-bedroom apartments with small kitchens

Small or large doses of anxiety

Soft cotton

A table crowded with food, booze, family, and friends

A cup of tea or coffee in your favorite mug

Salt, sand, and sun

Afternoon naps

Candles big and small

School lunches

A manhandled weekend paper

Breakfast

Impromptu visits

A warm breeze

Old-time jazz

Daydreaming

Pajamas

Valiant failures

Giddy love

Neglected vacuums

A cozy sweater

Vulnerability

Introduction:
For the Love of Cake

I've always loved cake. Deeply. The fewer ingredients a cake has, the more I want it. There's nothing as comforting as the smell of a cake baking when you walk into a home. It smells like love.

Simple Cake is a selection of unfussy, classic recipes that I've been tinkering away at for years, not only to satisfy cravings but also to share my love of cake with my family and friends. These recipes are the ones that are in high rotation in my busy home. They're simple enough to survive a little household chaos; in fact, let's just agree that pandemonium is one of the ingredients.

Because no two cravings are the same, I've written this like a choose-your-own-adventure cake book: ten cakes and fifteen toppings that can be mixed and matched to create endless flavor combinations. At their simplest, these cakes can be baked and dusted with confectioners' sugar. I've also created a chart of flavor combinations for you to experiment with as you get to know the recipes. Following the base recipes are thirty cake-worthy moments when the people in my life need or enjoy cake, and it goes way beyond birthdays.

You might be wondering where to find the time and energy to bake a cake. It's hard enough most days just getting dinner on the table; right? But here's the thing; I promise you that it won't take long to bake one of these cakes for that birthday boy or girl, for a friend who's having a rough time, for yourself as a bribe, for someone who has captured your heart, for a family treat, or because it's rainy and you're stuck inside with sick kids. Bake for the people you love, and they'll surely love you for it. Baking a cake for someone shows that you've put them at the forefront of your mind, that you've used your time and creativity to love them. Even if it's lopsided love.

I had the idea for *Simple Cake* rattling around in my head for years. There's an iconic publication that had a huge impact on my relationship with cake:

The Australian Women's Weekly Children's Birthday Cake Book. Published in the eighties, it became the bible for kids' parties around the country and a cult classic back home in Australia. The premise was simple: one cake recipe, a handful of toppings, and a bunch of fanciful themed designs that made it nearly impossible for a child to choose just one every year. You wanted them all so badly that the selection process became half the fun. There were typewriters, pools, rockets, castles, pirates, and the coveted train cake that graced the cover. (I never got that one!) These cakes satisfied every kid's birthday cake dream. It was an imaginative workhorse of a book—home-baker friendly and a source of rich family folklore. Making the cakes generated many happy and hilarious memories. It was always exciting to turn up at a friend's birthday party to see which cake they had chosen and how their family had executed the design.

It was the unexpected death of my father that finally gave life to *Simple Cake*. When I was back in Australia helping organize Dad's funeral, I found myself poring over his old photos. In among the curling images was one of Dad and me. We're in the backyard with a neighborhood friend and my brother. I was dressed in Dad's paint-splattered cargo work shirt, looking at a cake he had baked for my birthday, taken from a recipe in *The Australian*

Women's Weekly Children's Birthday Cake Book. Dad is craning over the cake, lighting the candles as I helped by shielding them. Despite the fact that my father's family had owned a successful bread bakery in town, I know that Dad, a newly divorced father in his late thirties, would have been out of his comfort zone baking a bunny birthday cake. It was a bittersweet discovery, a happy childhood memory I'd forgotten about that I suddenly wished I could thank him for.

That photo was taken more than thirty years ago, and I'm now a mother to Opal and Ned and stepmother to their big sisters Dixie and Matilda. Remembering that cake my father had created made me appreciate how important small acts of kindness are in the big picture, that when you step outside your comfort zone, good things can transpire. I'm now a long way from that secure, suburban childhood. Twelve years ago, I left Australia for love, and it has been an adventure. Home is now a brownstone in Brooklyn with a never-ending rotation of friends and family coming and going. I love the energy of a full house. It keeps homesickness at bay and gives me a good excuse to bake. After I returned home from Dad's funeral, I felt a need to share why I believe cake matters.

Simple Cake started with a summer of baking and jotting down my cake memories. (Tough gig.) My infatuation with cakes began, as it does for many, in early childhood. On special occasions, my mother would bake, and after she had finished mixing the batter, my brother and I would each get a beater to lick. One beater was never enough. I'd sneak my fingers into the batter when she wasn't looking and rescue the spatula from the sink. When I was a little older, I'd come home from school craving something sweet. When I couldn't find anything except the salty sandwich spread, Vegemite, and brown bread in the pantry, I'd mix myself some cake batter. I did this so often that I memorized a basic batter recipe—with just the perfect afternoon portion. Most times, I wouldn't bother baking the cake—I'd just eat the batter. To this day, I still don't know which I love more: the batter or the baked cake. I have no fear of salmonella.

My daughter Opal has inherited this cake gene. When she was young, she always wanted to help me bake. Help might not be the most accurate verb here. In the delirious years when the kids were little, I baked a lot of cakes to keep my spirits and energy high. This is how my business began. I wanted a simple, beautiful apron for Opal to wear while she was pottering around the kitchen with me, and since nothing on the market fit the bill, I made one for her. Friends then wanted one for their kids, and eventually I founded a business, OW Brooklyn, based on my designs.

Even if you didn't grow up baking at your mother's side or if baking isn't usually your thing, you can easily tackle the recipes in this book. I completely understand that baking can be intimidating, but I've worked hard to take some of that fear away. In *Simple Cake*, I've left out the cakes that can give even me heart palpitations, like the chiffon, angel, sponge, roll, and genoise. I promise you don't have to be an expert baker to bake what I give you here. You're more than qualified and, over time, your confidence will grow.

There's theater in baking, and that's what makes it fun. No two bakes are ever the same, and I guarantee there will be off days. Even when a recipe becomes an old friend, it reserves the right to surprise. You'll learn how to make assessments as you bake. Every time I make one of these recipes, somehow my muscle memory allows me to bake it with more fluidity because I've gone through the motions of those exact steps before. I enjoy recognizing the nuance between bakes and knowing what tweaks I might need to make. Some days the batter may look a little thick, so I'll add a dash of liquid, or the oven might be running hot, and I'll adjust the temperature accordingly. Some of my best cakes have happened when I allow myself a moment to relax and just bake without a ticking clock.

There's a modesty and nostalgia to these cake recipes. They're not extravagant, with tottering towers and layer upon layer of cake and buttercream. To be honest, when I see those kinds of cakes, I can appreciate the craftsmanship, but I have little desire to eat them. Give me a slice of heavenly warm cake, straight from the oven and impatiently cut anyday. I'm completely okay with the topping sliding off my slice.

So, friends, put on your aprons, and let's get baking. Remember: even if it doesn't look as good as you had hoped, who cares? There's no difference between a styled cookbook photo and your slightly crooked cake when it comes to taste and joy. Over time, you may even commit a few recipes to memory. There is no failure in having a go. *Simple Cake* is all about a return to simple pleasures and the relationships in your life that matter. I hope this book finds its way into your home, that it gets dog-eared and stained, and that your family and friends fondly remember the cakes you bake. For me, it has been a trip back to my childhood to say "Thank you and good-bye" to Dad.

Ingredients.

eggs.
milk.
flour.
baking powder.
honey.
butter.
confectioners sugar.
ice cream.
cream.
vanilla.

Let the Baking Begin!

The recipes in this book are my family's go-tos. They're the cakes I enjoy baking, and that we all enjoy eating. They're not extravagant—not too rich or complex—and above all, they're easy and quick to make. These are the flavors that get requested time and time again. Opal wants lemon, Dixie meringue, Matilda chocolate, and Ned needs vanilla.

With these cakes, toppings, and variations, you'll have all you need to bake classic, tasty recipes. They will become the building blocks for endless creativity. The Chocolatey Chocolate Cake, Cinnamon Spice Cake, Tangy Olive Oil Cake, Versatile Coconut Cake, Lovely Lemon Cake, and Madeleines can all be made without a mixer. A novice baker or a child, with some assistance, can easily pull them off. The others require basic beating, but for the most part, I'm trying to get that cake in your mouth as soon as possible.

At their simplest, the ten cake recipes in the first chapter can be dusted with confectioners' sugar. Amen! But if you want toppings, there are many ways to go, and I give you fifteen options for mixing and matching in the next chapter. My favorite combinations are in the Flavor Chart (page 178), but if you want Toblerone Ganache instead of Nana's Simple Glaze on your Very Vanilla Cake, knock yourself out. In the last chapter I give you thirty ideas for going beyond just mixing and matching with decorating and flavor ideas for any occasion that calls for cake. My hope is that you make these recipes and ideas your own to nourish your family and friends.

A Note about Cooking with Kids

I'm often asked if I have any advice for cooking with kids. (How about a stiff drink?) It requires the patience of a grandparent, and you have to surrender some control. Kids are going to make a mess—get flour in the cinnamon jar, scatter sugar on the floor, spill the good vanilla, and drop eggshell in the batter. Their dirty fingers will touch everything, including the sofa you just will have cleaned. They might even decide to have a meltdown in the middle of things, for no reason at all. I'm feeling your pain already.

It's tough to enjoy baking with kids when they're really young. You're mostly occupied with finding activities to keep them busy. If the thought of baking with them is too daunting, just set them up on the floor with some pots, pans, and utensils to bang on while you bake. Just seeing a parent cook, especially for pleasure and comfort, is a gift.

As kids get a little older, you can introduce them to cooking through the foods they've grown to love. I haven't yet met a kid who doesn't like cake, so one of these recipes is a good place to start. Let the child choose the cake, write a shopping list together, and make going to the supermarket to get the ingredients an outing. I have fond memories of sleeping at my aunt's house and her teaching me to how to make schnitzel. I stood on a stool, and she showed me how to pound the meat, coat it with flour, dip it in egg, and then cover it with bread crumbs. I learned a cooking technique I still use often, but more important, I experienced the joy of cooking with a loved one and eating something scrumptious that we'd made together.

My children are a little older now, and they're starting to find their way around our kitchen independently. They can even do the not-so-fun stuff such as unpack the dishwasher. As I worked on *Simple Cake*, Opal, who is ten, made her own cookbook by printing out recipes she'd found on the internet and then putting them in a recipe binder my stepmother had given her. She writes notes or draws pictures next to her recipes, just as I do. She wants to do everything by herself without any help. I grit my teeth when I see lumpy batter or an overfilled pan leaking in the oven. Cleanup is still a battle, but she beams with pride and confidence even when the finished product looks like a volcanic catastrophe.

My teenage stepdaughters, Dixie and Matilda, often ask if we can bake something when they're with us. Matilda is better at math than I am, so she helps me work out volume and scaling calculations for the cake recipes. Needless to say, she is a precise baker. Dixie, being the eldest, leads and tames the little kids while calmly making her way through a recipe. She introduces us to new music while she bakes and doesn't forget to pull the cake out of the oven. Ned just wants to crack the eggs and lick the bowl.

Over the years, there have been tears and tantrums, of course, but baking has helped the kids with their reading, math, and writing. It has taught them to follow a recipe and to recognize and appreciate ingredients. So pour yourself that drink, put on a great playlist, and surrender. This is a long-term investment.

ADVICE FROM THIS HOME BAKER TO ANOTHER

These small tips and tricks will make your bake the best it can be.

Follow the recipe. Read the recipe first and then begin baking. This seems obvious, but it's worth saying.

Set your oven rack. Remove the bills you've been hiding from and set the oven rack in the middle.

Preheat your oven. If the oven isn't up to temperature when the cake goes in, the cooking time will change, and your cake might not be as glorious.

Don't open your oven during baking. Wait until the second half of the bake; open the door only if you absolutely must. Work quickly, as the change in temperature can affect the quality of your bake.

Use recommended pan sizes. I've provided multiple options for each cake recipe. These are the pans the cakes shine in.

Prepare your pans. Grease, add parchment paper, and grease again. It's an insurance policy.

Expiration dates. Check the expiration dates of all ingredients, especially the baking powder!

Prepare all ingredients. I'm guilty of not always doing this, but I'm getting much better at it. Doing this saves time and limits mistakes. It's easy to omit an ingredient or forget whether or not you've already added it. Eek!

Bring ingredients to room temperature. If you've forgotten to bring the eggs out of the fridge, place them in a bowl of warm water to get them there faster. To soften butter, dice it or very gingerly use the microwave.

Melted butter only works when it's called for. You should be able to press your finger into the butter and leave a slight imprint. Err on the side of having the butter cooler, since the mixer will help soften it when you beat it.

Sift. Sifting aerates the flour so the cake is airy and light; sift the flour together with the leaveners, salt, and spices. Whisking first and then sifting will ensure that the leaveners are evenly distributed.

Avoid curdling the batter. When liquid is added to fat, such as adding eggs to creamed butter and sugar, the mixture can often curdle. To avoid this, you need to emulsify—adding the two ingredients to one another in small additions—so the ingredients get a chance to disperse properly. Start by whisking the eggs and then gradually adding them a tablespoon at a time to the butter mixture, beating well between each addition. The mixture may still curdle toward the end, but if this happens, don't panic. Although it may look as if things have gone awfully wrong, just add a tablespoon or two of the flour mixture to bind it all together again before proceeding.

Adjust batter that's too thick. If you were heavy-handed with the measuring of flour or let the batter sit around for too long, the batter can be thicker than it should be, making it difficult to pour. If the batter looks a little too thick or gluggy, add a tablespoon or two more of the liquid used in the recipe to loosen the batter. Smooth thicker batters before baking, so they rise evenly.

Drop the unbaked cake. No, don't drop it on the floor; that wouldn't be good. Just drop it a few inches down onto the kitchen counter before placing it in the oven to get rid of any large rogue air bubbles and to make sure that thicker batters are evenly distributed in the pan.

Set a timer (because you will forget). If you don't have a timer, use your cell phone. Set the timer for at least ten to fifteen minutes before the suggested bake time to check on the cake. Stick around the kitchen during the final ten minutes to make sure you don't overbake your cake. Having a glance in the first half never hurts.

Stop the cake from browning too quickly. Gently cover the top of the cake with aluminum foil.

Rotate the cake. If the cake is rising unevenly this will help it level out.

Check the cake is baked. Gently insert a wooden skewer or toothpick into the center of the cake and pull it out. If it's slightly greasy with the odd crumb, it's done. If it's wet, it's not. The cake should have pulled ever-so-slightly away from the pan . To be sure, gently press your finger down into the center of the cake; if it springs back and doesn't make an indent, it's done.

Rest the cake. After it comes out of the oven, let the cake sit in the pan on a wire rack for five to ten minutes to give it some time to ready itself for all the attention. Trying to get your masterpiece out of the pan too early might break it or cause the edges to tear off.

Release the cake. Run a butter knife around the edges and gently encourage the cake off the sides and bottom of the pan. Give the pan a jiggle—you're trying to ease the cake out before inverting it onto the cooling rack. Peel the parchment paper from the sides, then place the cooling rack on top of the baking pan. Invert cake. Peel the parchment off the bottom of the cake.

Stop the cake from sticking to the rack. Repurpose the used parchment paper from the bottom of the cake, and place it between the rack and the cake.

Store the cake. I try to avoid putting these cakes in the refrigerator, as refrigeration firms up the fat in the cake, making the texture dense. Use a glass cake dome, sealed plastic container, or plastic wrap instead and try to keep the cake at room temperature. If there's a heat wave, you can make an exception.

Freeze the cake. Honestly, I rarely do it because the cake never lasts that long. However, I can understand the time efficiency in baking a cake ahead of time and freezing it. Make sure to wrap the cake well in plastic wrap, sealing it from the air and any odors. Bring the cake out of the freezer in plenty of time to let it come to room temperature before serving.

Revive day-old cake. First, congrats that the cake lasted longer than a day. Sometimes, just to breathe new life into it, I'll pop a slice in the microwave and reheat it for 10 seconds or even better, grill it in butter in a small frying pan (page 105). It's ridiculously good; just don't tell your cardiologist.

TIPS FOR USING FLOUR

(1)

FLUFF THE FLOUR WITH
A SPOON OR WHISK TO AERATE.

(2)

SPOON THE FLOUR INTO A DRY
MEASURING CUP TO FILL IT.

(3)

LEVEL THE FLOUR USING THE
BACK OF A KNIFE.

(4)

DON'T COMPACT THE FLOUR BY
TAPPING, BANGING, SHAKING, OR
OVERPACKING THE MEASURING CUP.

(tip)

OVERPACKING THE CUP
WILL MAKE THE BATTER THICK
AND THE CAKE DRY.

Measuring and Weighing Ingredients

Here are my best practices for getting the right amount of everything, no matter what tools you have at your disposal.

DRY INGREDIENTS

Use standard stainless steel nesting measuring cups and spoons. Flat bottoms and straight handles make it easier to measure accurately. Make sure they are clean and dry before using.

LIQUID INGREDIENTS

Use glass measuring cups and get down to eye level because the meniscus (the curved upper surface of the liquid) can be deceptive.

DIGITAL SCALES

These really do make your baking life easier and offer a more precise way of baking. Digital scales don't cost a lot, and they rule out any margin for error. If you haven't used one before, it can feel intimidating, but once you get the hang of it and become familiar with the tare button, there will be no turning back. That said, for years I baked cakes successfully without owning a scale.

MEASURING WITHOUT A SCALE

The most finicky ingredient to measure without a scale is flour. I could have written an entire book about measuring flour, but for your sake and mine, I'm glad I didn't. The amount of flour you end up with in your cup depends on how you go about getting it into the cup. In the United States, many brands and types of flour are available on the market, each with its own characteristics and weight—another factor that can complicate the matter. *Simple Cake* calls 1 cup of all-purpose flour, 130 grams (4.5 ounces). I've settled on this number because from my experience, if you use the method of measuring flour listed opposite (that I use for all flour types), you will get the most consistent results— approximately 130 grams in each cup—without using a scale. All the recipes that use all-purpose flour have been tested to work for this weight of flour.

Basic Methods and Techniques

A cake can come together using various methods and techniques. Understanding and mastering these basics will make the simplest of cakes shine.

SIFTING

Sifting aerates the flour and helps distribute the leaveners, salt, and spices. I'll often whisk the dry ingredients together first and then sift them to be thorough. I sift the flour after it's measured by putting the flour, followed by the leaveners, salt, and spices, into a large 3-cup sifter, or large fine-mesh sieve. You can also sift the flour mixture onto a large sheet of parchment paper. Gather up the sides of the parchment and pour the flour into the batter. At first, this can feel clumsy, but it will get easier with practice.

COMBINING

It's as simple as making a box cake and requires no special equipment. Using a wooden spoon or whisk, stir wet ingredients into dry ingredients until the batter is smooth. Don't overbeat, since you will activate the gluten too much, making your cake tough. If you are new to baking, start with one of the cakes that uses the combining method, such as Chocolatey Chocolate Cake (page 22), Madeleines (page 50), Versatile Coconut Cake (page 42), Cinnamon Spice Cake (page 30), or Lovely Lemon Yogurt Cake (page 46).

CREAMING

You might be familiar with this method from making cookies. It involves gradually adding fine sugar to room temperature butter and beating to incorporate and trap air bubbles that will help the cake rise. An electric mixer is not essential, but to get a light, fluffy, aerated mixture, it really helps. When in doubt, beat the mixture longer than you think—no less than four minutes and up to eight minutes for larger cakes such as the Milk and Honey Cake (page 34). The mixture should look light, fluffy, and whitish in color. Test it by rubbing the mixture between your fingers; if the sugar feels very fine, you're good to go. The Very Vanilla Cake (page 26) and Milk and Honey Cake (page 34) employ the creaming method.

FOLDING IN

This method gently folds and cuts whisked egg whites or flour into a batter. Add egg whites to the mixture a third at a time. Use a large spatula to lift the batter from the bottom of the bowl and fold it over into the whites. Rotate the bowl continuously, slicing through the center of the batter often. Don't stir or you will knock all the air out of the egg whites—it's the air that helps make your cake rise. Repeat with each third until you have a lovely, airy batter. In the Almond Gató recipe (page 54), I reserve some of the nut flour to fold in at the end so that the batter isn't too stiff. This helps avoid knocking out air from the egg whites.

WHIPPING

Use a whisk, or an electric mixer with a whisk attachment, to whip egg whites or heavy cream. Make sure the equipment or utensils are completely clean and dry. The temperature of the ingredients and utensils is very important to successfully whip.

EGG WHITES

To whip egg whites, there must be absolutely no traces of fat in your whites or on the mixing bowl and whisk. I always wipe a splash of white vinegar over the bowl and equipment before I begin to eliminate all fat, because fat deflates egg whites. Humidity can make it tough, too.

My vote is to use fresh eggs at room temperature. A common mistake is to overwhip egg whites until they're dry and lumpy. Dry, lumpy egg whites will rob your cake or meringue of moisture. Note that when whipping egg whites for the Almond Gató (page 54), the peaks will be softer because of the absence of sugar. The Meringue (page 58), with the addition of sugar, makes stiffer peaks.

CREAM

I prefer to whip heavy cream by hand, even though it takes a little longer. This way I have more control. Make sure the cream, equipment, and utensils are clean and very cold. I'll often put the mixing bowl and whisk in the freezer for ten minutes before I whip the cream to chill them. Beat the cream until the mixture has more than doubled in volume, and soft, pillowy peaks plop off a spoon. If the cream starts to look like cottage cheese or slightly grainy, they're signs you've over beaten it.

MELTING

Use heat to change a solid ingredient to a liquid. This can be done in the microwave or in a double boiler—a metal or glass bowl that rests snugly above a saucepan of simmering water. Make sure the water doesn't touch the bottom of the bowl.

TEMPERING

There is no tempering of chocolate required in the Toblerone Ganache (page 80). However, tempering is required to make the Crème Anglaise (page 91). By gradually pouring the hot milk onto the egg and sugar mixture, while constantly whisking, you slowly bring the temperature of the two heat sensitive ingredients together. This technique stop the eggs from curdling.

Ovens and Baking Times

Ovens are just like people, they come in all shapes and sizes and have their own unique personality. Some ovens run hot; others have poor circulation or hot spots, and some have no oomph, like the old humdinger I use when we are at our vacation home on Fire Island. I highly recommend spending a couple of dollars to invest in a digital oven thermometer to get an exact temperature reading. Think of it like speed dating with your oven—it can shortcut the getting-to-know-you phase, helping you avoid heartbreak.

CONVENTIONAL VERSUS CONVECTION OVENS

I established the estimated bake times for *Simple Cake* using two types of ovens—a conventional oven and a convection oven (sometimes called fan-assisted or fan-forced oven) in bake mode. I love baking cakes in my conventional oven because it allows the cake to retain moisture by ensuring a slow rise that's golden. Convection ovens can often be ferocious. You will probably have to reduce the baking time if using a convection oven. If the cake is browning too quickly, turn the temperature down slightly. My suggested baking times are not gospel but guides. Set your timers, trust your instincts, and stay near your masterpiece during the final 15 minutes of baking.

Equipment and Pans

When I moved from Sydney to Manhattan more than ten years ago, I arrived with only a backpack full of clothes. I had shipped two boxes of my favorite books—but no baking tins. Since we were living in a one-bedroom apartment in Hell's Kitchen with limited storage and counter space, that was a good thing. Amy, my dearest and oldest New York friend, who loves cake as much as I do, gifted me a few essential baking tools (see list below). To say this set the friendship off on solid ground would be an understatement, since we have shared a lot of life and cake together since. You don't need a lot of gadgets to bake these cakes; even beaters aren't essential for many of the recipes. Later on you may want to invest in good beaters and other baking equipment. Or you could do what another friend did one morning and just use your hands as beaters. Whatever it takes. Cake is cake is cake is cake.

EQUIPMENT LIST

Two large bowls (glass, metal, or ceramic work well)

Large metal balloon whisk

Wooden spoon

Standard stainless steel nesting measuring cups and spoons

Large glass Pyrex measuring cup

Large rubber spatula

Large sifter or a sieve

Wire rack

Two 8- or 9-inch round baking pans

Cupcake pan

TYPES OF PANS

I prefer sturdy anodized aluminum pans. They're durable and bake with a consistent heat, browning the cake evenly. They heat and cool fast so the cake doesn't overcook after being taken out of the oven. These pans are more expensive, but the bake is much better than what you'll get from other pans. Be sure to wash them by hand and not in the dishwasher. I like Nordic Ware pans, especially the ornate Bundts; Fat Daddio's has a wide selection of quality pans, too.

PREPARING YOUR PANS: AN INSURANCE POLICY

This is my least favorite part of baking, yet I'm a stickler for doing it. The most foolproof way to avoid swearing and to aid the cake's safe exit is to grease the pan, line the bottom and sides with parchment paper, and grease the paper. Sure it adds another five minutes to your prep time, but if you've just spent an hour baking a cake, why take any chances having the cake get stuck, broken, or overcooked around the edges? You can sometimes just grease and lightly dust the pan with flour; just promise me you will do it my way on the Milk and Honey Cake (page 34) and the Very Vanilla Cake (page 26). For specialty pans such as Bundts, madeleines, and financier trays, generously grease each cavity with butter using your fingers and then lightly dust with flour and shake off any excess.

10
Cakes

THE ONLY CAKES YOU'LL EVER REALLY NEED

These ten cakes can stand a little chaos. In my experience, there's wiggle room with these recipes, unless you double down on the baking soda or forget the sugar. That's why I implore you to take a swipe of the batter before you put it in the oven to make sure it tastes good. If it tastes delicious before it goes in, chances are, it will remain that way. And what's the worst that can happen? You overbake it, and it dries out. Nothing a lashing of whipped cream can't remedy.

(1) Chocolatey Chocolate Cake

This cake is pure celebration and my chocolate go-to. Not too rich but ridiculously moist, it is decadent without being overly sweet. It's almost impossible to mess up and so easy to make; it gives Betty Crocker a run for her money. If you have a whisk and two large bowls, you can pull this off. Since the batter is very runny, avoid using a springform pan, which can leak. This cake is a slight adaptation of my dear friend Simon's recipe. He effortlessly cooks for thirty people without breaking a sweat, and everything he makes tastes delicious—including this cake. There's also an added bonus: the final product has some serious shelf life—it will keep fresh for days, and it freezes well if you would like to bake it ahead of time.

**Makes one 10 by 3-inch
round cake
Preparation: 20 minutes**

. . . .

1¾ cups (225g) all-purpose flour

½ cup (45g) unsweetened Dutch-
processed cocoa powder

1½ teaspoons baking powder

1½ teaspoons baking soda

½ teaspoon salt

1½ cups (300g) granulated sugar

2 eggs, at room temperature

1 cup (240ml) whole milk

½ cup (120ml) grapeseed oil or
any mild-flavored oil

½ teaspoon pure vanilla extract

1 cup (240ml) boiling water

Preheat the oven to 350°F. Grease a 10 by 3-inch round pan with butter, line the bottom and sides of the pan with parchment paper, and grease the paper. (I'll let you just grease, line the bottom of the pan, and lightly flour the sides if you're feeling lazy.)

Place a large sifter or a sieve in a large mixing bowl. Add the flour, cocoa, baking powder, baking soda, and salt and sift.

Add the sugar and whisk until combined.

In another large bowl, whisk the eggs, milk, oil, and vanilla together.

Gradually add the wet ingredients to the dry ingredients and whisk until there are no lumps and the batter is smooth.

Carefully pour in the boiling water and stir until combined. (Watch the little ones with the hot water!)

Pour the batter into the prepared pan. Bake in the center of the oven for approximately 50 minutes or until a wooden skewer inserted in the center comes out clean, and the cake bounces back when lightly pressed.

Remove from the oven and let the cake stand for 10 minutes. Run a butter knife around the cake to gently release. Peel off the parchment paper from the sides. Invert the cake, peel off the bottom piece of parchment, and cool on a wire rack.

Tip

You can double this recipe when it's party time—just use a 15 by 11-inch sheet pan and bake for 35 to 40 minutes.

VARIATION

Coffee Enhanced Chocolate Cake: Swap the cup of water for a cup of hot black coffee.

TOPPINGS

- Dust with confectioners' sugar.
- Swirl the top with Chocolate Swiss Meringue Buttercream (page 88), then add a sprinkle of fleur de sel or Maldon salt
- Poke holes in the top of the cake and then soak with Tres Leches (page 81). Chill and then serve with Condensed Milk Whipped Cream (page 75).
- Spoon warm Toblerone Ganache (page 80) or Caramel Sauce (page 92) over a warm slice or into individual Chocolatey Chocolate Cakes baked in small ramekins. Make sure to scoop vanilla ice cream on top, too.
- Smother in Silky Marshmallow Icing (page 87) for a sweet black and white cake.
- Dust with confectioners' sugar and then put a dollop of Coffee Whipped Cream (page 75) or Nutella Whipped Cream (page 75) on the side.
- Bake with Chocolate Crumble (page 77) and serve warm with a scoop of vanilla ice cream.

TRY THESE OTHER OPTIONS

Two 8- or 9-inch round pans. Bake for 35 to 40 minutes.

One 12 by 8-inch or 13 by 9-inch rectangular pan. Bake for 25 to 30 minutes.

10 to 12 individual ramekins (grease and fill halfway). Bake for 20 to 25 minutes.

Two 12-cup cupcake pans (fill liners no more than halfway). Bake for 20 to 25 minutes.

(2) Very Vanilla Cake

A basic vanilla cake was the first cake recipe I mastered and memorized. Over the years, I've tinkered away at this old-school-flavored recipe, making tweaks here and there to make this modest cake a little special. There are a few little extra steps and ingredients involved, but I believe they are worth the trouble. The seeds of a vanilla bean combined with extract really pump up the vanilla-y flavor. The sour milk (an acid) combined with the dash of baking soda (an alkaline) creates a wonderfully soft, fluffy crumb. I especially love making it in a sweet six-inch springform pan. This cake is best eaten on the day it's made; in fact, I'll often bust out 12 cupcakes on a whim if I know friends with kids are coming. Even with the extra steps, it's that easy to make.

Makes one 6 by 3-inch round cake
Preparation: 25 minutes

. . . .

2 teaspoons freshly squeezed lemon juice

½ cup (120ml) whole milk

2 eggs, at room temperature

Scraped seeds of 1 vanilla bean

¾ cup (150g) granulated sugar

1½ cups (195g) all-purpose flour

1 teaspoon baking powder

¼ teaspoon baking soda

¼ teaspoon salt

8 tablespoons (1 stick/115g) unsalted butter, at room temperature

1 tablespoon plus 2 teaspoons pure vanilla extract

3 tablespoons grapeseed oil or any mild-flavored oil

Preheat the oven to 350°F. Grease a 6 by 3-inch springform pan with butter, line the bottom and sides with parchment paper, and grease the paper.

Add the lemon juice to the milk to sour it. Set aside for 5 to 10 minutes or until curdled.

In a small bowl, whisk the eggs together. Set aside.

In another small bowl, use your fingers to work the vanilla bean seeds into the sugar. Remove any bits of pod that may have come off with the seeds. Set aside.

Place a large sifter or a sieve in a large mixing bowl. Add the flour, baking powder, baking soda, and salt and sift.

Using an electric mixer with beaters or a paddle attachment, beat the butter for 30 seconds on medium speed and then gradually add the sugar. Scrape down the sides of the bowl. Continue beating on medium speed for another 4 minutes or until light in color and fluffy.

Add the vanilla extract and beat until combined.

With the mixer still on medium speed, gradually add the eggs. If the batter curdles, add 1 to 2 tablespoons of the flour to bind it back together.

On low speed, add the flour mixture and then the oil and milk; mix until just combined. Don't overbeat. Scrape down the sides and bottom of the bowl.

Pour the batter into the prepared pan and smooth the top. Bake in the center of the oven for 50 to 55 minutes. Cover the top of the cake with tinfoil after 30 minutes so the cake doesn't take on too much color. When a wooden skewer inserted into the center comes out clean, and the cake bounces back when lightly pressed, remove the cake from the oven and let it stand for 10 minutes. Run a butter knife around the cake to gently release. Peel off the parchment paper from the sides. Invert the cake, peel off the bottom piece of parchment, and cool on a wire rack.

Tips

To get the cake you truly deserve, sift the flour mixture twice to get the flour as aerated and light as possible, or give it a spin with cake flour.

The keys to this cake being moist are not to overpack the measuring cup with flour and not to overbake it.

If you are making mini cupcakes watch them carefully, especially if you are using aluminum-lined cupcake papers. They hold the heat and can easily overcook the cupcakes.

You can double this recipe when it's party time—just use two 8 by 2-inch round pans for a layer cake.

If you don't have vanilla beans in your pantry, increase the vanilla extract to 2 tablespoons.

VARIATIONS

Berry Vanilla Cake: Lightly dust 1 cup (130g) of raspberries or 1 cup (140g) blueberries with flour, then gently fold into the batter.

Funfetti Vanilla Cake: Omit the vanilla bean and add ¼ cup (50g) of rainbow sprinkles. (Don't use rainbow nonpareils, since they'll dissolve too quickly in the batter, and you won't get that pop of color.) Gently fold the sprinkles into the finished batter. If the batter thickens, add 1 to 2 tablespoons of milk.

TOPPINGS

- Dust with confectioners' sugar. (A paper stencil works great for a simple decoration on an 8 by 2-inch cake.) Serve with slightly warm Compote (page 83) and Vanilla Whipped Cream (page 75).
- Decorate cupcakes with Easy Creamy Icing (page 72), Mascarpone Easy Creamy Icing (page 72), or Beautiful Buttercream (page 73).
- Drizzle with Nana's Simple Glaze (page 70).

TRY THESE OTHER OPTIONS

One 8 by 2-inch round pan. Bake for 35 minutes.

One 8 by 3-inch Bundt pan. Bake for 30 minutes.

One 12-cup cupcake pan (fill liners two-thirds full). Bake for 17 to 20 minutes.

One 48-cup or two 24-cup mini cupcake pans (fill liners two-thirds full). Bake for 12 to 14 minutes.

(3) Cinnamon Spice Cake

This cake is like having a hot apple-cider-donut truck in your kitchen. The smell of cinnamon and sugar baking will draw people to your front door. This recipe is not overly spiced and keeps for days; in fact, I think it's better on the second day when the flavors have had time to rest. This is a healthy-ish fall cake that can easily be whipped together. It is deserving of a pair of slippers, a cardigan, and a cup of tea.

Makes one 13 by 9-inch
rectangular cake
Preparation: 20 minutes

2¼ cups (270g) organic whole-grain
spelt flour

1½ teaspoons baking powder

½ teaspoon baking soda

½ teaspoon salt

1 teaspoon ground cinnamon

½ teaspoon ground nutmeg

3 eggs, at room temperature

½ cup (120ml) mild-flavored
extra-virgin olive oil

1 teaspoon vanilla extract

1 cup (240g) unsweetened
applesauce

¼ cup (85g) honey

½ cup (120ml) whole milk

1 tablespoon finely grated
orange zest

1 cup (190g) light brown sugar,
lightly packed

Preheat the oven to 350°F. Grease a 13 by 9-inch rectangular pan with butter, line the bottom and sides of the pan with parchment paper, and grease the paper. (I'll let you just grease, line the bottom of the pan, and lightly flour the sides if you're feeling lazy.)

Place a large sifter or a sieve in a large mixing bowl. Add the flour, baking powder, baking soda, salt, cinnamon, and nutmeg and sift.

In another large bowl, whisk the eggs, oil, vanilla, applesauce, honey, milk, zest, and brown sugar until smooth.

Gradually add the wet ingredients to the dry ingredients and whisk until there are no lumps and the batter is smooth.

Pour the batter into the prepared pan and smooth the top. Bake in the center of the oven for 28 to 30 minutes or until a wooden skewer inserted in the center comes out clean, and the cake bounces back when lightly pressed.

Remove the cake from the oven and let it stand for 10 minutes. Run a butter knife around the cake to gently release. Invert the cake, peel off the parchment paper, and cool on a wire rack.

Tip

You can double this recipe when it's party time—just use a 15 by 11-inch sheet pan and bake for 30 to 35 minutes.

VARIATIONS

Walnut Spice Cake: Add ½ cup (55g) of walnuts or pecans, toasted and roughly chopped, to the batter. Dust the nuts with a little flour before adding to the batter to stop them from sinking to the bottom.

Ginger Spice Cake: Add ½ teaspoon of ground ginger and ½ teaspoon of ground allspice to make the cake more aromatic.

TOPPINGS

- Dust with confectioners' sugar. (A paper stencil works great for a simple decoration.)
- Brush the top of the cake with melted butter and then sprinkle with Cinnamon Sugar (page 172) for some donutlike crunch.
- Frost the cake with Cream Cheese Frosting (page 76) and sprinkle with roughly chopped toasted walnuts or pecans.
- Serve warm with Caramel Sauce (page 92) and a scoop of walnut ice cream.

TRY THESE OTHER OPTIONS

One 10 by 3-inch round pan. Bake for 40 to 45 minutes.

Approximately 10 mini individual Bundts (fill tray cavities two-thirds full). Bake for 20 to 25 minutes.

Two 12-cup cupcake pans (fill liners two-thirds full). Bake for 18 to 20 minutes.

4 Milk and Honey Cake

Very subtle, not overly sweet, slightly tangy, and so delicate.
I promise you that peeling the buttery, sweet disk of parchment
paper off this cake will be a glorious moment. I'm a sucker for
a jar of artisanal honey, so I often play around baking this cake
using different flavor-infused honeys such as sage, lavender,
thyme, and ginger. Don't be tempted to bake the whole batter
in one pan. This cake shines when it has less time in the oven.
That's why I divide it between pans or bake cupcakes that require
less baking time. Because of the honey, make sure you line the
bottom and sides of the pans with parchment paper to stop the
exterior of the cake from taking on too much color and sticking
to the sides, creating crumbly edges. Milk and Honey cupcakes
topped with Mascarpone Easy Creamy Icing (page 72) is a
scrumptious combination.

Makes two 8 by 2-inch round cakes
Preparation: 25 minutes

2¼ cups (290g) all-purpose flour

2 teaspoons baking powder

½ teaspoon baking soda

¼ teaspoon salt

3 eggs, at room temperature

1 cup (240ml) buttermilk, shake carton

¾ cup (255g) honey

½ teaspoon pure vanilla extract

12 tablespoons (1½ sticks/170g) unsalted butter, at room temperature

¾ cup (150g) granulated sugar

Preheat the oven to 350°F. Grease two 8 by 2-inch round pans with butter, line the bottom and sides of the pans with parchment paper, and grease the paper.

Place a large sifter or a sieve in a large bowl. Add the flour, baking powder, baking soda, and salt and sift.

In a small bowl, whisk the eggs together. Set aside.

In another small bowl, whisk together the buttermilk, honey, and vanilla. Set aside.

Using an electric mixer with beaters or a paddle attachment, beat the butter for 30 to 45 seconds on medium speed, then gradually add the sugar. When all the sugar has been added, stop and scrape down the sides of the bowl with a spatula. Continue beating on medium speed for another 4 minutes or until light in color and fluffy.

With the mixer still on medium speed, add the eggs 1 tablespoon at a time, over 3 minutes. If the batter curdles, add 1 to 2 tablespoons of the flour to bind it back together.

With the mixer on low speed, add the dry and wet ingredients alternately two times, starting and ending with the dry. Mix until just combined and smooth. Don't overbeat. Scrape down the sides and bottom of the bowl with a spatula to make sure it's well combined.

Pour the batter into the prepared pans and smooth the top. Bake in the center of the oven on the same rack for 35 to 38 minutes or until a wooden skewer inserted in the center comes out clean, and the cake bounces back when lightly pressed.

Remove the cakes from the oven and let them stand for 10 minutes. Run a butter knife around the cakes to gently release. Peel off the parchment paper from the sides. Invert the cakes, peel off the bottom piece of parchment, and cool on a wire rack.

Tips

To get the cake you truly deserve, sift the flour mixture twice to get the flour as aerated and light as possible, or give it a spin with cake or spelt flour.

The keys to this cake being moist are not to overpack the measuring cup with flour and not to overbake it.

To make one cake, halve the ingredients. To divide an egg, simply crack the egg into a small bowl, whisk, and use a tablespoon to measure half.

VARIATIONS

Ginger Milk and Honey Cake: Add 1½ teaspoons of ground ginger to the flour mixture.

Lavender Milk and Honey Cake: Put 2 to 3 teaspoons of edible lavender and the granulated sugar into a food processor and grind until lavender is finely ground.

TOPPINGS

- Dust with confectioners' sugar and drizzle each slice with a little honey or add a dollop of Honey Whipped Cream (page 75).
- If you are making cupcakes, promise me you'll smear them with Mascarpone Easy Creamy Icing (page 72).
- Fill the center of a layered cake with Honey Whipped Cream (page 75) and top with strawberries for a marvelous rendition of a classic Victoria sandwich cake.

TRY THESE OTHER OPTIONS

Two 9-inch round pans. Bake for 30 to 35 minutes.

Two 12-cup cupcake pans (fill liners no more than halfway). Bake for 20 to 22 minutes.

(5) Tangy Olive Oil Cake

Honestly, this cake is a killer. It's sophisticated, yet good for young
and old, day or night. If you're looking for a daytime pick-me-up
or a simple dessert for your next dinner party, here it is. The hint
of citrus brightens up the cake and accentuates the fruitiness of
the extra-virgin olive oil. I remember when I was a kid, I didn't
like the texture of rind, so to this day, I grate mine finely using a
Microplane. If your olive oil smells too herbaceous and savory,
reach for a milder, buttery, extra-virgin olive oil instead. Buttermilk
isn't usually found in olive oil cakes, but I find it a welcome addition,
adding tang and helping to fluff the rich crumb. This cake can be
made by hand using a whisk if you don't have an electric mixer.
For a simple dessert, dust a pretty pattern on a cooled cake with
confectioners' sugar and serve with a dollop of Yogurt Whipped
Cream (page 75) and a glass of chilled sparkling Moscato d'Asti.
If you have any leftovers, that's breakfast.

5

TANGY OLIVE OIL CAKE, continued

Makes two 8 by 2-inch round cakes
Preparation: 20 minutes

. . . .

2 cups (260g) all-purpose flour

1 tablespoon baking powder

½ teaspoon salt

3 eggs, at room temperature

1⅓ cups (265g) granulated sugar

¾ cup (180ml) mild-flavored extra-virgin olive oil

½ cup (120ml) whole milk

½ cup (120ml) buttermilk, carton shaken before measuring

¼ cup (60ml) freshly squeezed orange juice

1 tablespoon finely grated orange zest

Preheat the oven to 350°F. Grease two 8 by 2-inch round pans with olive oil or butter, line the bottom and sides of the pans with parchment paper, and grease the paper. (If using individual Bundt pans or fluted cupcake pans, grease them generously with butter, using your fingers to get into all the grooves, and then lightly dust with flour, shaking off any excess.)

Place a large sifter or a sieve in a large mixing bowl. Add the flour, baking powder, and salt and sift.

Using an electric mixer with beaters or a paddle attachment, beat the eggs and sugar on medium speed until pale and aerated, about 3 minutes. Scrape down the sides of the bowl with a spatula. Add the oil, milk, buttermilk, juice, and zest. Continue beating on low speed until combined and frothy like a milkshake, about 1 minute.

Gradually add the wet ingredients to the dry ingredients and whisk or beat until just combined and smooth.

Pour the batter into the prepared pans.

Bake in the center of the oven on the same rack for 30 to 33 minutes or until a wooden skewer inserted in the center comes out clean, and the cake bounces back when lightly pressed.

Remove the cakes from the oven and let them stand for 10 minutes. Run a butter knife around the cakes to gently release. Peel off the parchment paper from the sides. Invert the cakes, peel off the bottom piece of parchment paper, and cool on a wire rack.

Tips

• Avoid using deeper pans that require a longer time to bake. They make it tricky to assess whether the cake is baked through, since the exterior can look golden, and a skewer can even come out clean, but the interior still needs to bake a little longer.

• If you are using fluted cupcake pans, pull them out of the oven before they become golden (the sides take on color quickly because of the thin metal pans).

VARIATIONS

Citrus Olive Oil Cake: Substitute lemon, lime, or maybe grapefruit for the orange juice and zest.

Chocolate-Orange Olive Oil Cake: Substitute ½ cup (45g) of unsweetened Dutch-processed cocoa powder for ½ cup (65g) of flour.

TOPPINGS

• Dust with confectioners' sugar. (A paper stencil works great for a simple decoration.)
• Serve each slice with a dollop of something such as White and Whipped Cream (page 75). I especially like Yogurt Whipped Cream (page 75). Add Compote (page 83) or fresh berries.
• Ice cupcakes or Bundts with Nana's Simple Glaze (page 70) for a lovely finish.
• Serve cake slices or individual Bundts with Crème Anglaise (page 91), topped with toasted flaked almonds.

TRY THESE OTHER OPTIONS

Approximately 12 mini individual Bundts (fill tray cavities two-thirds full). Bake for 20 to 25 minutes.

Two 12-cup cupcake pans (fill liners three-quarters full). Bake for 18 to 20 minutes.

One 24- or two 12-cavity fluted cupcake pans (fill two-thirds full). Bake for 17 to 20 minutes.

⑥ Versatile Coconut Cake

My wedding cake was a coconut cake, so this flavor makes me sentimental. This recipe is an adaptation of my stepmother's cake, which I've always loved and find ridiculously easy to make. No beaters needed here. For the simplest version, sprinkle shredded coconut over the greased baking pan before baking for a little crunch on the exterior of the cake, and dust with confectioners' sugar when cool. Or try the decadent chocolate variation, pictured at right. Put the kettle on, and promise me that one day you'll have a slice while it's still warm, or better yet, pan-fried in butter (page 105).

6

VERSATILE COCONUT CAKE, continued

Makes one 8 by 2-inch round cake
Preparation: 20 minutes

. . . .

1 cup (130g) all-purpose flour

1 teaspoon baking powder

¼ teaspoon salt

1 cup (70g) fine dried shredded
unsweetened coconut

¾ cup (150g) granulated sugar

2 eggs, at room temperature

⅔ cup (160ml) well-stirred
unsweetened coconut milk

8 tablespoons (1 stick/115g) unsalted
butter, melted

Preheat the oven to 350°F. Grease an 8 by 2-inch round pan with butter, line the bottom and sides of the pan with parchment paper, and grease the paper. Alternatively, grease the pan and dust with coconut, shaking off any excess.

Place a large sifter or a sieve in a large mixing bowl. Add the flour, baking powder, and salt and sift.

Add the coconut and sugar to the flour mixture and whisk to combine.

In a small bowl, whisk together the eggs and coconut milk.

Gradually add the wet ingredients to the dry ingredients and stir until combined.

Finally, add the melted butter and stir until smooth.

Pour the batter into the prepared pan and smooth the top. Bake in the center of the oven for 30 to 35 minutes or until a wooden skewer inserted in the center comes out clean, and the cake bounces back when lightly pressed.

Remove the cake from the oven and let it stand for 10 minutes. Run a butter knife around the cake to gently release. Peel off the parchment paper from the sides. Invert the cake, peel off the bottom piece of parchment paper, and cool on a wire rack.

Tips

• If you are making mini cupcakes watch them closely, especially if you are using aluminum-lined cupcake papers. They hold the heat and can easily overcook the cupcakes.

• You can double this recipe when it's party time—just use a 10- to 15-cup Bundt pan.

VARIATIONS

Raspberry Coconut Cake: Gently fold in 1½ cups (195g) of raspberries into the batter.

Coconut and Cardamom Cake: Add ¼ to ½ teaspoon of ground cardamom to the flour mixture.

Chocolate Coconut Cake: Substitute ¼ cup (20g) of unsweetened Dutch-processed cocoa powder for ¼ cup (30g) of the flour. Whisk and sift the cocoa into the flour mixture.

TOPPINGS

• Dust with confectioners' sugar.
• Drizzle with Coconut Glaze (page 70) and sprinkle toasted shaved coconut.
• Serve with Compote (page 83) and Vanilla Whipped Cream (page 75).
• Generously top with Vanilla Whipped Cream (page 75), shaved semisweet chocolate, and toasted shaved coconut.
• Ice cupcakes with Cream Cheese Frosting (page 76) and top with roughly chopped, toasted macadamia nuts or shaved coconut.

TRY THESE OTHER OPTIONS

One 9 by 5-inch loaf pan. Bake for 50 minutes.

One 8 by 3-inch Bundt pan. Bake for 30 minutes.

One 10½ by 7½-inch rectangular ceramic dish. Bake for 30 minutes.

One 12-cup cupcake pan (fill liners two-thirds full). Bake for 17 to 20 minutes.

One 48-cup or two 24-cup mini cupcake pans (fill the liners half full). Bake for 12 to 14 minutes.

⑦ Lovely Lemon Yogurt Cake

I've always loved the combination of lemon and yogurt in my cakes. One bowl and a whisk are all you need to make this lovely, nurturing cake that makes everyone happy. I've adapted this recipe from the French classic *gâteau au yaourt*. I understand that it is one of the few cakes the French bake at home. If you have a petit chef, this is the perfect recipe to introduce them to baking.

7

LOVELY LEMON YOGURT CAKE, continued

Makes one 9 by 5-inch loaf cake
Preparation: 20 minutes

2¼ cups (290g) all-purpose flour

3 teaspoons baking powder

½ teaspoon salt

2 eggs, at room temperature

¾ cup (180ml) grapeseed oil or any mild-flavored oil

1 cup (230g) plain Greek full-fat yogurt

Finely grated zest of 1 large lemon

⅓ cup (80ml) freshly squeezed lemon juice

1 cup (200g) granulated sugar

Preheat the oven to 350°F. Grease a 9 by 5-inch loaf pan with butter, line the bottom and sides of the pan with parchment paper, and grease the paper.

Place a large sifter or a sieve in a large mixing bowl. Add the flour, baking powder, and salt and sift.

In another large bowl, whisk the eggs, oil, yogurt, zest, lemon juice, and sugar until combined.

Gradually add the wet ingredients to the dry ingredients and whisk until there are no lumps and the batter is smooth.

Pour the batter into the prepared pan and smooth the top. Bake in the center of the oven for 50 to 55 minutes. Cover the top with tinfoil after 30 minutes if it's browning too quickly or turn the oven down slightly.

When a wooden skewer inserted in the center comes out clean, and the cake bounces back when lightly pressed, remove the cake from the oven and let it stand for 10 minutes. Run a butter knife around the cake to gently release. Peel off the parchment paper from the sides. Invert the cake, peel off the bottom piece of parchment paper, and cool on a wire rack.

Citrus Yogurt Cake: Substitute lime, orange, blood orange, or ruby grapefruit for the lemon.

Poppy Seed Yogurt Cake: Fold 2 tablespoons of poppy seeds into the batter.

Berry Yogurt Cake: Sprinkle huckleberries, blueberries, raspberries, blackberries, or a combination on the top of the batter and gently push them in. Alternatively, fold flour-dusted berries into the batter.

Berry Crumble Yogurt Cake: Sprinkle Berry Crumble (page 77) on top of the batter and bake in a 10-inch springform pan for 50 to 55 minutes.

TOPPINGS

- Dust generously with confectioners' sugar.
- Drizzle with Nana's Simple Glaze (page 70), substituting freshly squeezed lemon juice for the water or milk.
- Prepare a Lemon Syrup (page 78) or Gin Syrup (page 78). Use a toothpick to poke deep holes in the cake an inch apart, then spoon the syrup over the top of the cake, letting it soak in gradually.
- Serve slightly warm with Yogurt Whipped Cream (page 75) or ice cream.
- Slice the 9-inch round cake horizontally through the center to make two layers and slather with Compote (page 83) or Raspberry Curd (page 84) and Yogurt Whipped Cream (page 75). Dust the top of the cake with confectioners' sugar.
- For cupcakes, scoop out a small teaspoonful of cake from the center of each cupcake and dollop in Raspberry Curd (page 84). Spoon or pipe Silky Marshmallow Icing (page 87) on top to be decadent.

TRY THESE OTHER OPTIONS

One 9 by 2-inch round pan. Bake for 40 to 45 minutes.

Three 6-cup cupcake pans (fill liners two-thirds full). Bake for 18 to 20 minutes.

⑧ Madeleines

Buttery, light, and not overly sweet, madeleines are dead-easy to make. The only thing that stopped me from making them for years was not owning a madeleine pan. I don't know why I waited so long. Do yourself a favor, splurge and get two pans so you can crank out more than one batch at a time. We recently shared a special birthday dinner with good friends at Daniel Boulud's eponymous restaurant in New York City, and at the end of the meal, the waiter brought freshly baked mini madeleines all bundled up for dessert. They were still warm and lightly dusted with confectioners' sugar, and we gobbled them up in minutes. Madeleines can be made without beaters and are best eaten on the same day as close to the bake as possible.

I was impressed that the pastry chef at Daniel had managed to get a good hump in the middle of the mini madeleines. Personally, I prefer regular-sized madeleines without a hump, unless I'm putting curd into their bellies. If you're all about the hump, make sure you leave the batter in the fridge for at least an hour to chill before baking, and pop the greased and dusted madeleine pans in the freezer while you're preparing the batter; the chill will help the madeleines rise in the center.

MADELEINES, continued

Makes 20 madeleines
Preparation: 20 minutes, plus 1 hour for the batter to chill in the fridge

. . . .

1 cup (130g) all-purpose flour

1 teaspoon baking powder

¼ teaspoon salt

2 eggs, at room temperature

½ cup (100g) granulated sugar

½ teaspoon pure vanilla extract

2 tablespoons honey or golden syrup (see Tips)

½ teaspoon lemon or orange zest

8 tablespoons (1 stick/115g) unsalted butter, melted

Preheat the oven to 350°F. Prepare the madeleine pans by greasing each shell generously with butter, getting into all the nooks and crannies, then lightly dust with flour or, if making the chocolate variation, dust with cocoa. Tap off any excess. Place the prepared pans in the freezer for at least 10 minutes.

Place a large sifter or a sieve in a large mixing bowl. Add the flour, baking powder, and salt and sift.

In a small bowl, whisk together the eggs, sugar, vanilla, honey, and zest.

Gradually add the wet ingredients to the dry ingredients and whisk until there are no lumps.

Finally, add the melted butter and whisk until smooth.

Pour the batter into a ziplock bag or cover the mixing bowl tightly with plastic wrap. Chill the batter for an hour in the fridge.

Cut a corner off the ziplock bag or spooning the batter, fill each shell about one-half full, approximately 1 level tablespoon per shell. The batter will have thickened, so gently drop and tap the tray on the kitchen counter to encourage it into the grooves. The batter will flow beautifully into the shells in the heat of the oven.

Bake for 8 to 10 minutes. The edges will have pulled away slightly from the shell and be golden. Be careful not to overcook, which can happen quickly.

Let the madeleines sit for 5 to 10 minutes; then, using a butter knife, gently nudge them out of the pans. Cool on a wire rack.

Tips

Golden syrup is not as common a baking ingredient here in the United States as it is in Australia and the United Kingdom. It is made from cane sugar and gives a lovely warmth and sweetness to baked goods. Look for it in the baking aisle at specialty supermarkets like Whole Foods Market. I use Lyle's Golden Syrup.

The batter can be made the day before and kept in the refrigerator.

VARIATIONS

Chocolate Madeleines: Replace 2 tablespoons of flour with 2 tablespoons of unsweetened Dutch-processed cocoa powder. Use orange zest, not lemon zest. Bake for approximately 8 minutes. Dust the finished madeleines with a mix of cocoa and confectioners' sugar. For a dinner party dessert, you might serve these with a half-quantity of the decadent warm Toblerone Ganache (page 80). The flecks of the nougat in the Toblerone are a nice addition to the soft cakes. You can have your friends spoon the ganache on top of the madeleines or dip them in it like fondue.

Hazelnut Madeleines: Substitute ½ cup (65g) of the all-purpose flour with ½ cup (45g) of hazelnut meal or flour. Just whisk the dry ingredients, because the meal is difficult to sift. Use orange zest, not lemon zest. These require a very thorough greasing of the pan and are difficult to get a hump from, but they taste yummy. Bake for approximately 8 minutes. Dust with confectioners' sugar or dip them in warm Toblerone Ganache (page 80). Make a half-quantity of the ganache, since only the tips get dipped.

Citrus Curd Madeleines: After the madeleines have cooled slightly, place cooled Raspberry Curd, or any of the curd variations (page 84), into a piping bag. Use a small metal piping tip to gently poke a hole into the belly of the madeleine and inject curd until you can see it. Or I'm completely down with simply serving a spoonful of curd on the side. Sprinkle with confectioners' sugar just before serving.

TOPPINGS

- Dust with confectioners' sugar.
- Dip the tips of the madeleines into Nana's Simple Glaze (page 70).

9 Almond Gató

This is an elegant, gluten-free delight. The magic of this cake comes when you bite into the soft cake and get a mouthful of the crunchy nuts that top the cake. After traveling to Spain I fell in love with this native Mallorcan cake, as both Claudia Roden and Rick Stein have before me. After lots of experimenting, I discovered the success of this cake is in the process more than the ingredients (see tip, page 57). The gató is different from other cakes in this book because beaten egg whites are gently folded into the nut–flour mixture to make the cake rise. It's quite common for cakes that use egg whites as the leavener to slightly drop in the center after they come out of the heat of the oven. Make a virtue of this trait and don't invert the cake, but instead fill the dip with delicate flaked nuts and dust with confectioners' sugar. I use superfine almond flour for a fine crumb or almond meal for a rustic vibe. Be sure to try the Hazelnut Gató variation too!

9

ALMOND GATÓ, continued

Makes one 9 by 2-inch round cake
Preparation: 25 minutes

- -

6 eggs, at room temperature
1 cup (200g) granulated sugar
1 teaspoon pure vanilla extract
A few drops of pure almond extract
Finely grated zest of 1 lemon
1¾ cups (160g) almond meal or flour
½ teaspoon salt
¾ cup (65g) flaked almonds, toasted

Preheat the oven to 350°F. Grease a 9 by 2-inch round pan with butter, line the bottom and sides of the pan with parchment paper, and grease the paper—a must for this cake.

Separate the egg yolks and whites into two medium mixing bowls.

Using a whisk or an electric mixer with beaters or a paddle attachment on medium speed, beat the egg yolks and the sugar for 2 minutes or until very pale, ribbonlike, and aerated. Add the vanilla and almond extract and the zest. Beat for another minute. Scrape down the sides of the bowl with a spatula.

Add 1 cup (90g) of the almond meal or flour and the salt. Mix until just combined; don't overbeat.

In the other bowl, use the whisk attachment and whisk the egg whites on medium-low speed for 2 minutes, until small, even bubbles form. Gradually increase the speed to medium-high and beat for another 2 minutes, or until firm peaks form.

Heap a spoonful of the whipped egg whites into the almond mixture. Using a spatula, lift the mixture from the bottom of the bowl and fold it over, gently incorporating the whites to loosen the mixture. Add the remaining egg whites a third at a time. Rotate the bowl continuously, slicing through the center of the mixture often. Don't stir; you will knock all the air out.

Finally, gently fold in the remaining ¾ cup (70g) of almond meal or flour.

Pour the batter into the prepared pan and gently smooth the top. Bake in the center of the oven for 30 to 35 minutes or until a wooden skewer inserted in the center comes out clean, and the cake bounces back when lightly pressed.

Remove the cake from the oven and let it stand for 10 minutes. Run a butter knife around the cake to gently release. Peel off the parchment paper but do not invert. Cool on a wire rack.

To top the cake, toast the flaked almonds on a baking sheet in the oven or in a frying pan over low heat until lightly colored and aromatic. Sprinkle the nuts on top of the cooled cake and dust with confectioners' sugar.

Tip

The folding-in technique can be intimidating. I get it! One really valuable tip I learned from my mother is to reserve ¾ cup (70g) of the nut flour until the end. This way the mixture won't be as stiff, making it easier to fold in the egg whites without knocking the air out of them. If it's a humid day, consider making a different cake, since whipped egg whites struggle in humid weather.

VARIATIONS

Hazelnut Gató: I love this variation! Use hazelnut meal or flour in place of almond meal or flour. Omit the almond extract and the lemon zest; use orange zest instead. Top with roughly chopped toasted hazelnuts instead of the almonds and dust with confectioners' sugar.

Cinnamon Almond Gató: Add ½ teaspoon of ground cinnamon to the batter.

Boozy Almond Gató: To take this cake into the evening, add 1 tablespoon of Grand Marnier or Amaretto to the almond mixture before folding in the egg whites.

TOPPINGS

- Dust with confectioners' sugar.
- Serve with grilled or poached apricots and a scoop of vanilla gelato in the summertime. Or top with a dollop of Boozy Whipped Cream (page 75), using Grand Marnier.
- Serve with a spoonful of Compote (page 83) and Vanilla Whipped Cream (page 75).
- Hazelnut Gató loves Nutella Whipped Cream (page 75). Top the cake with toasted, chopped hazelnuts and a dollop of cream on the side. If you love the combination of hazelnut and chocolate, try adding shaved semisweet chocolate to the topping as well; be sure to let the hazelnuts cool before adding. (See also the Holiday Hazelnut Cake on page 153.)

(10) Meringue

This is not technically cake, but it's equally as celebratory, as well as being a great option for family members who might not be so enamored with cake. It's also a great gluten-free option. A bowl of white glossy meringue with stiff peaks is a glorious sight. After years of experimenting, I've settled on a six-egg meringue, which makes a robust Pavlova or individual meringues that have a crisp shell and a marshmallow interior. Be sure to read my tips on page 61 before you begin, since meringue is one of those simple recipes that can sometimes be temperamental. The recipe can easily be halved for more modest midweek individual meringues.

**Makes 1 large Pavlova or 8 to
10 (2½-inch) individual meringues
Preparation: 20 minutes**

. . . .

**1½ cups (300g) caster or
granulated sugar**

**1 teaspoon white vinegar, plus
a splash for wiping utensils**

6 egg whites, at room temperature

2 teaspoons cornstarch

**1 teaspoon pure vanilla extract
(optional)**

Preheat the oven to 300°F.

Line a large flat baking tray with parchment paper. Draw guides by tracing around an 8-inch round cake pan for a Pavlova or use a 2½-inch cookie cutter for the individual meringues. Flip the parchment paper upside down so the marking doesn't end up on the meringue.

If you are using granulated sugar, grind it in a food processor or put it in a ziplock bag and crush with a rolling pin, until it's fine, like caster sugar.

Wipe a little vinegar over the whisk attachment and the mixing bowl of an electric mixer to make sure it's free from any fat residue. Add the egg whites to the bowl, making certain there is no yolk.

Beat the egg whites on low speed, gradually increasing the speed to medium. Beat until the egg whites have soft peaks, about 4 minutes. Add the cornstarch. Increase the speed to medium-high and, without stopping the mixer, gradually add the sugar a tablespoon at a time. Continue beating until the meringue is smooth, glossy, and tripled in volume.

Finally, add the teaspoon of vinegar and the vanilla and mix until just combined.

Dollop a finger of meringue in the corners of the tray to secure the paper. Using the circle or circles you have traced as your guide, pile the meringue high onto the center of the circle or circles. Using a spatula or a spoon, gently work the meringue to fit the circle and create a slight indentation in the center.

Turn the oven temperature down to 250°F. Place the baking tray in the center of the oven. For the Pavlova, bake for approximately 1 hour and 20 minutes or until the outside is crisp and the center soft. For the individual meringues, bake for approximately 40 minutes; check on them after the first 10 minutes to make sure they're not browning too much. If they are, turn the oven down a little bit more.

When meringue has baked, turn off the oven. Leave the tray in the oven to cool completely. Remove the Pavlova or individual meringues from the oven just before serving.

Tips

· Meringue needs fine sugar, such as caster sugar.

· Meringue hates fat; keep those yolks out of the whites.

· Meringue likes boundaries and enough volume to create a crisp outside and a soft center.

· Meringue loves to be cooked low and slow.

· Meringue deflates in humidity and cracks with abrupt changes in temperature.

· Meringue is friends with Crème Anglaise (page 91) and Raspberry Curd (page 84), so use up those yolks.

VARIATIONS

Vanilla and Chocolate Swirl Meringue: Make the meringue. Place half of the meringue in a clean bowl. Sift ⅓ cup (30g) unsweetened Dutch-processed cocoa powder into this half. Don't stir, but gently fold in the cocoa—it doesn't have to be fully incorporated. The fat in the cocoa will slightly deflate the meringue, so work quickly and gently. Using two dessert spoons, take a generous spoonful of both the chocolate and vanilla meringue. Dollop them together within the round guides you've drawn. To make a pretty nest, use a teaspoon to smooth the perimeter of the meringue and then gently press the top of the meringue with the back of the teaspoon, flicking the wrist to create a small indentation and perky peaks. You need enough meringue to give you the crispy exterior but a soft center. (Remember that meringue expands in the oven.) The mounds should all be roughly the same size so they take the same time to bake.

Eton Mess: An Eton Mess is a great solution for a not-so-successful meringue. Break the meringue into serving bowls and smother it in White and Whipped Cream (page 75) and berries.

Flavored and Colored Meringue: Experiment with flavoring the meringue before it is baked; use essences like hazelnut and almond, or fold in ground nuts, crushed dehydrated fruit, or ground cinnamon. Vanilla bean paste is also wonderful. You can also use food coloring sparingly to tint the meringue.

TOPPINGS

· Dress individual meringues with Crème Anglaise (page 91), raspberries, and toasted almonds.

· Top with White and Whipped Cream (page 75) and serve with seasonal fruit, a dollop of chilled Raspberry Curd (page 84), or warm Compote (page 83) during the cooler months.

· Shaved chocolate, crushed nuts, or flaked coconut add extra crunch to meringues.

15

Cake Toppings

THE PERFECT FINISH TO YOUR CAKE

Toppings can be luxurious showstoppers or simple, subtle additions that provide balance, texture, flavor, and color. Toppings should never overpower. I'm deeply suspicious when I see mountains of buttercream. Although I have been known to use toppings to cover unexpected glitches, I don't want them to hide the beauty of the bake. A small golden glimmer peeking out from the perimeter of the cake can prepare the mouth and mind for what's coming. The topping recipes that follow go beyond buttercream. They can be swirled, smeared, poured, spooned, crumbled, dolloped, injected, soaked, or scooped onto the cake or served on the side.

SIMPLE WAYS TO TOP A CAKE!

There are many extravagant ways to decorate a cake, but I'm all about simple touches that give a cake personality that's unique to the occasion or the recipient.

Confectioners' Sugar and Homemade Stencils

Dusting a cake with confectioners' sugar is the quickest way to top a cake. It's perfect for those times when you've just come home from work and discovered you need to bust out a cake. I like seeing some of the naked cake that's often hidden by icing. Dusting confectioners' sugar over a stencil is a fun way to pretty and personalize a cake. I have also used edible glitter and colored dust. Fall leaves or other simple shapes like stars make easy stencils. Hold the stencil on the cake and dust the cooled cake just before serving as the confectioners' sugar will dissolve over time.

Personalized Typographic Stencils

You don't have to be a graphic designer to pull this off. These can be done freehand for a looser feel or using a computer if you want to be more exact. Think about stenciling birth years, ages, monogram initials, song lyrics, or perhaps a proposal. If you do create the stencil on a computer, choose a simple, bold, sans serif font that will be easy to read and cut out. Make sure you scale it so it fits the size of the cake. It helps to print the stencil on a thicker card stock to get defined lines around the letters. You'll need a surface you can cut the stencil on, like a cutting mat, and an X-Acto knife and ruler. It helps to score the letters first to get clean, precise cuts around each letter. Cut out each letter. Hold the stencil securely down on the cake and use a fine-mesh sieve to dust confectioners' sugar over each letter. When you've

finished, lift the stencil carefully off the cake without knocking the letters you've stenciled.

Parchment Paper Stencils

Making stencils from parchment paper is just like cutting out snowflakes in school at holiday time. Kids love making these, and I think they look charming strung up as party decorations. Trace the bottom of the baking pan onto the parchment paper. Using scissors, cut out the perimeter. Fold the paper into four equal sections: half, then quarters, then eighths. Cut out shapes from the paper, leaving the curved outer edge free from cuts. Open out the folded paper. Hold the stencil securely down on the cake and use a fine-mesh sieve to dust confectioners' sugar over the stencil. When you've finished, lift the stencil carefully off the cake.

A Pop of Color and Crunch

Fresh fruit, dehydrated fruit, chopped nuts, shaved chocolate, toasted coconut, infused sugars, and flaky salt all add flavor, color, and texture to the top of a cake. Sprigs of herbs and edible flowers are dreamy, and sprinkles are natural cheerleaders.

Candles, Cake Toppers, and Collectibles

I've always got my eyes peeled for special candles, miniature vintage toys and figurines, and other cake toppers. Over the years, I've collected some gems that I've found in gift and stationery stores, flea markets, and on Etsy and eBay. I enjoy rummaging through my collection when I need to match a cake with a topper. I feel delight when I reconnect with the ones I've forgotten. It's the same feeling I used to get as a child opening the Christmas decorations every year.

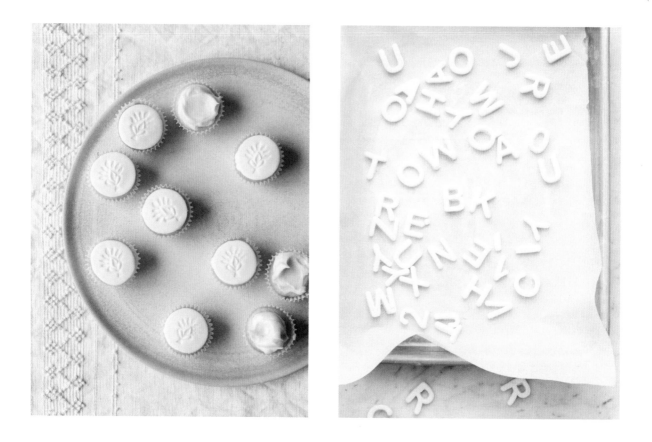

Fun with Fondant

Fondant can provide a bit of fun for both kids and adults because it's like edible Play-Doh. It can be colored with food dye, drawn on using gourmet edible markers, imprinted with food-safe stamps, or cut into shapes and letters. Although it's often used to blanket a cake, I prefer to use thin fondant accents on mini cupcakes. They're easier to work with and lend themselves to playful decoration. Fondant is expensive, so using it sparingly is economical and doesn't compromise the flavor of the cake. Available at specialty cooking stores or online, fondant comes in various colors and flavors; however, I prefer to buy white vanilla fondant and tint it myself to achieve subtler tones. Both Satin Ice and Wilton sell white vanilla fondant.

Tips for Working with Fondant

• Work fondant between your hands to make it malleable before you roll it out.

• Always keep fondant covered since it dries out quickly if left uncovered.

• Fondant is best prepared and eaten on the same day. However, you can prepare shapes and disks the night before as long as you store them in airtight containers. Separate any layers with both parchment paper and plastic wrap to stop them from sticking to one another and from drying out.

• Use food-safe edible stamps or edible gourmet food markers to decorate the fondant.

• Cakes with fondant still need a layer of icing for added flavor and adhesion. Don't put the fondant on prematurely, since it gradually softens on contact with the icing.

Nana's Simple Glaze

A glaze is one of the quickest ways to add a complementary flavor to the top of a cake. Feel free to play around with the flavors and the consistency of your glaze. A Bundt needs a glaze that clings to its decorative shape, so you don't want it too runny, Madeleines should dip effortlessly into a runny glaze. Loaf cakes want glaze to crisscross over their cracks and crevices.

Makes approximately ½ cup; enough for one 9 by 5-inch loaf cake or 6 by 3-inch round cake
Preparation: 5 minutes

1 cup (115g) confectioners' sugar
1 tablespoon unsalted butter, softened
2 tablespoons boiling water

Sift the confectioners' sugar into a small mixing bowl. Make a well in the center of the sugar and add the butter. Pour the boiling water onto the butter to melt it. Stir the sugar, butter, and water together until smooth. If you prefer a runnier consistency, just add a bit more water.

TIP: For a glaze that clings, err on the side of it being thicker. Pour the glaze continuously onto the center of the cake, so that the glaze evenly distributes. Less is more. You don't want too much pooling.

VARIATIONS

Citrus Glaze: Replace the boiling water with the freshly squeezed juice of a lemon, orange, lime, blood orange, or grapefruit, according to your taste. Adjust the consistency by adding a little more juice. Add finely grated zest to boost the flavor.

Berry Glaze: Throw in a handful of raspberries and use the back of a spoon to slightly mash them into the glaze for a bright, messy affair. Save a few berries to garnish the top of the cake.

Passion Fruit Glaze: Replace the boiling water with fresh passion fruit juice—with seeds or sans seeds; it's up to you.

Vanilla Glaze: Add ½ teaspoon of pure vanilla extract, and/or the scraped seeds of ⅓ vanilla bean.

Coconut Glaze: Omit the butter. Instead of the boiling water, add 3 to 3½ tablespoons of unsweetened coconut milk, shaken and stirred. Add enough coconut milk to reach your preferred consistency.

(2)

Easy Creamy Icing

This is dead easy—simply add cream to confectioners' sugar. This icing is soft and loose, so it works well using only a smear. It lives between a glaze and a buttercream. For Little Treasures (page 127), I cover the top of the cake with this icing and let it drape over the edge. You can play around with the consistency by adding more liquid or more confectioners' sugar. This icing is suited for smaller surface areas and can be easily colored.

Makes ¾ cup; enough for one 8-inch round cake or 12 cupcakes
Preparation: 5 to 10 minutes

1½ cups (170g) confectioners' sugar
¼ cup (60ml) heavy cream
¼ teaspoon pure vanilla extract

Sift the confectioners' sugar into a medium bowl. Pour in the cream and the vanilla and stir with a wooden spoon until smooth. Use an offset spatula or a butter knife to ice the top of the cake, or use the back of a dessert spoon to smear onto cupcakes.

VARIATION

Mascarpone Easy Creamy Icing: Replace the heavy cream with ½ cup (115g) mascarpone for a tangy Easy Creamy Icing. Beat the mascarpone and confectioners' sugar until smooth. You may want to add 1 teaspoon of finely grated lemon zest, too. This is a delightful icing to accompany the delicate Milk and Honey Cake cupcake variation (page 37). I guarantee you'll have a new go-to in your repertoire once you take a bite.

Beautiful Buttercream

Buttercream can overpower a cake if it's obnoxiously piled on top, disrupting the entire ratio of cake to topping. Buttercream also has a reputation for being sickly sweet. This is a beautiful buttercream, since the mascarpone and zest add a welcome tang that cuts through the sweetness. If you want to get fancy and pipe the buttercream onto the cake, you may want to add a little more confectioners' sugar to make a stiffer consistency.

Makes 1½–1¾ cups; enough for one 8-inch round cake or 12 cupcakes
Preparation: 10 to 15 minutes

2¾ cups (310g) confectioners' sugar

4 tablespoons (55g) unsalted butter, softened

¼ cup (55g) mascarpone

1 teaspoon finely grated lemon zest (optional)

¼ teaspoon salt

1 teaspoon pure vanilla extract

3 tablespoons whole milk

Sift the confectioners' sugar into a small bowl.

Using an electric mixer with beaters or a paddle attachment, combine the butter and mascarpone. Add the lemon zest. Beat on medium speed until creamy. Add the salt. Gradually add 2 cups of the sugar and beat until combined. Stop and scrape down the sides of the bowl with a spatula. Add the vanilla and the milk. Beat for about a minute and then add the remaining ¾ cup of the sugar and continue beating until smooth and creamy.

VARIATIONS

Passion Fruit Buttercream: Reduce the milk to ½ tablespoon and add 3 to 4 tablespoons of strained passion fruit juice.

Blueberry Buttercream: In a heavy saucepan, add ¼ cup (175g) of blueberries and 1 tablespoon of water. On low to medium heat, stir and burst the blueberries with the back of a wooden spoon. Cook for approximately 10 minutes or until the sauce has thickened a little. Strain through a sieve and let cool completely. Then add the blueberry juice in place of the milk as the liquid to the buttercream. The blueberry flavor is hard to detect, but it's a natural way to color the buttercream, and the hue is magnificent.

Chocolate Buttercream: Replace 5 tablespoons (35g) of the confectioners' sugar with 5 tablespoons (25g) unsweetened Dutch-processed cocoa powder and omit the zest.

White and Whipped Cream

If you have a slice of cake with a dollop of whipped cream on top, it's a good day. Whipped cream is quick to make, is not overly sweet, and it's the perfect accompaniment to cake. Dusting a cake with confectioners' sugar and serving it with whipped cream is often my first choice. I prefer to whip cream by hand, since there's less chance of overbeating, which can happen easily if distractedly using beaters. Whipping cream by hand makes you feel as if you've earned your cake and a few cheeky spoonfuls, too! Look for soft, pillowy peaks that plop off the spoon right into your mouth.

Makes approximately 2 cups; enough for one 10-inch round cake, 1 Pavlova, or 8 to 10 individual meringues
Preparation: 10 minutes

1 cup (240ml) heavy cream, chilled

Pour the cream into a cold large metal bowl. If adding any flavoring (see below), add it now. Using a balloon whisk, begin to whisk the cream until it has doubled in volume, has smooth soft peaks, and is light and fluffy.

VARIATIONS

Vanilla Whipped Cream: Add 1 teaspoon of pure vanilla extract and 1 tablespoon of confectioners' sugar.

Honey Whipped Cream: Add 2 tablespoons of honey.

Nutella Whipped Cream: Add 4 tablespoons of Nutella.

Yogurt Whipped Cream: Substitute ½ cup (120ml) of the heavy cream with ½ cup (115g) of plain Greek yogurt. Add 1 tablespoon of sifted confectioners' sugar. Add some finely grated zest for a delicious tang.

Condensed Milk Whipped Cream: Add 3 tablespoons of sweetened condensed milk.

Coffee Whipped Cream: Add 1 tablespoon of instant coffee and 2 tablespoons of confectioners' sugar.

Boozy Whipped Cream: Add 1 tablespoon of confectioners' sugar and 2 tablespoons of a spirit or liqueur. (I like Grand Marnier, Cointreau, or Frangelico.) Remember: you can always add more to taste but you can't take out extra!

Cream Cheese Frosting

**Makes 2 cups; enough for one
10-inch round cake or 24 mini cupcakes
Preparation: 10 to 15 minutes**

2 cups (230g) confectioners' sugar

8 tablespoons (1 stick/115g) unsalted
butter, at room temperature

1 cup (225g) cream cheese, at room
temperature

1 teaspoon pure vanilla extract

1 tablespoon pure Grade A maple syrup
(optional)

⅛ teaspoon of salt

Let's be honest: The cream cheese frosting is the best part of a carrot cake.
I also love it on the Cinnamon Spice Cake (page 30) or on top of the
Versatile Coconut Cake cupcake variation (page 42).

Sift the confectioners' sugar into a small bowl.

Using an electric mixer with beaters or a paddle attachment, combine the
butter, cream cheese, and vanilla. Add the maple syrup. Beat for a minute
or two on medium speed until well combined and creamy. Stop and scrape
the sides of the bowl with a spatula. Continue beating on low speed and
gradually add the confectioners' sugar and salt. Scrape the sides again
and then continue to beat until creamy and smooth, about 1 to 2 minutes.

Berry Crumble

Baking crumble onto the top of the cake adds a buttery crunch and frees you from having to ice the cake. A handful of roughly chopped walnuts or pecans are also a great addition to both the Berry and Chocolate Crumble. Bake cakes with crumble in lined springform pans so they're easy to release or in individual ramekins. Did I mention that warm crumble loves ice cream?

**Makes approximately 1½ cups;
enough for one 10-inch round cake
or 6 individual ramekins
Preparation: 10 to 15 minutes**

½ cup (65g) all-purpose flour

¼ cup (45g) light brown sugar,
lightly packed

½ teaspoon salt

4½ tablespoons cold unsalted
butter, diced

2 cups (280g) blueberries

In a large bowl, combine the flour, brown sugar, and salt. Add the butter and work it between your fingers until you have pea-size crumbles. Gently fold in the blueberries.

With the cake batter already in the prepared pan, sprinkle the crumble on top of the batter. Bake according to the recipe's directions, adding a few minutes more to the suggested baking time. If the top is browning too quickly, turn the oven down slightly or cover the top of the cake with tinfoil. Bake until lightly browned, crisp, and a wooden skewer inserted into the center of the cake comes out clean.

VARIATION

Chocolate Crumble: Replace the light brown sugar with 3 tablespoons of granulated sugar. Add 1½ tablespoons unsweetened Dutch-processed cocoa powder. Replace the blueberries with ⅓ cup (55g) semisweet chocolate chips.

Citrus Syrup

Syrups are an easy way to amp up the flavor of a cake and keep it moist for days. After you've put the cake in the oven, have the syrup simmering in a saucepan on the stove while you're cleaning up. Once the cake is out of the oven, keep the cake in the pan and poke holes into the cake with a skewer, then slowly spoon or brush the syrup evenly over the cake, giving it time to gradually soak in. You may like to play around with infusing syrups with herbs from the garden. I could eat the Lovely Lemon Yogurt Cake (page 46) with Gin Syrup (see below) for days. Come to think of it, I have.

**Makes ¼ to ½ cup, depending on preferred thickness; enough for one 9-inch round cake or loaf cake
Preparation: 10 to 15 minutes**

⅓ cup (80ml) freshly squeezed lemon or lime juice
¼ cup (50g) granulated sugar

In a heavy saucepan over low heat, stir the juice and sugar together until the sugar has dissolved. (The longer the syrup simmers, the more it will reduce and thicken.) For a syrup that really soaks into a cake, keep it reasonably runny. For a thicker, glossier finish that sits more on top of a cake, cook the syrup for 10 minutes. Stir the mixture often to make sure it doesn't smoke or burn.

VARIATIONS

Passion Fruit Syrup: Add the additional juice of 2 or 3 passion fruits—with or without seeds, your choice—to the Citrus Syrup and then cook.

Gin Syrup: Add ¼ cup (60ml) of gin to the Citrus Syrup after it's off the heat. Stir until combined.

Lavender Syrup: Add 2 tablespoons of edible dried lavender to the Citrus Syrup mixture and then cook. Strain syrup through a sieve before soaking cake.

Thyme Syrup: Add a few sprigs of fresh thyme to the Citrus Syrup mixture and then simmer. Strain syrup through a sieve before soaking cake.

Toblerone Ganache

This simple ganache is a riff on a Nigel Slater recipe. Instead of using the dark chocolate Toblerone, as he does, I use the traditonal milk chocolate one, so even the kids are happy. This ganache is perfect for dipping the Chocolate or Hazelnut Madeleines (page 53) into. Be sure to try the Chocolate Sour Cream Ganache Frosting variation below, too. It's my stepmother's recipe, which has frosted every sibling's chocolate birthday cake for the last forty-something years.

**Makes approximately 1 cup; enough for 10 to 12 individual ramekins, or 24 madeleines
Preparation: 10 minutes**

One 7½-ounce bar milk chocolate Toblerone

1 tablespoon unsalted butter, at room temperature

½ cup (120ml) heavy cream

¼ teaspoon pure vanilla extract

Break the Toblerone bar into individual triangles and place in the top of a double boiler. Bring an inch of water to a gentle simmer in the bottom of a double boiler and melt the chocolate and butter. Then turn off the heat and stir in the heavy cream and vanilla.

VARIATION

Chocolate Sour Cream Ganache Frosting: Replace the Toblerone with 1 cup (170g) of semisweet chocolate chips. Omit the butter. Melt the chocolate. Remove from the heat and add ¾ cup (170g) of sour cream instead of heavy cream. Add the vanilla, stirring until smooth.

TIP: You can melt the chocolate in the microwave on low or medium heat if you prefer. Just make sure to do it incrementally, stirring the chocolate in between intervals. If you over cook chocolate, it will look thick and lumpy.

9

Tres Leches

The name of this cake translates to "three milks": evaporated milk, condensed milk, and whole milk (or in this recipe heavy cream). Anything that has condensed milk in it has already won my heart. Tres Leches is so simple and it transforms a cake into a puddinglike dessert. I often reserve a little of the condensed milk and whip it into some heavy cream to serve on top of the cake.

Makes 3½ cups; enough for one 13 by 9-inch cake
Preparation: 10 minutes

One 12-ounce (355ml) can evaporated milk
One 14-ounce (395ml) can sweetened condensed milk
1 cup (240ml) heavy cream
Scraped seeds of 1 vanilla bean (optional)

In a large bowl, combine the evaporated milk, condensed milk, and heavy cream. Add the vanilla bean seeds and whisk together.

Cover with plastic wrap and refrigerate if not using immediately.

While the cake is still in the pan, use a skewer to poke holes in the top of the cake. Spoon the milk mixture over the top of the cake, giving it time to gradually soak into the cake. Cover the cake with plastic wrap and refrigerate overnight or for at least 5 to 6 hours.

VARIATIONS

Chocolate Tres Leches Cake: Soak the Chocolatey Chocolate Cake (page 22) in Tres Leches. Reserve a little condensed milk and make Condensed Milk Whipped Cream (page 75) and top the cooled cake with the cream. Sprinkle shaved semisweet chocolate on top.

Coconut-Cardamom Tres Leches Cake: Double the recipe for the Versatile Coconut Cake (page 42). Grind the seeds from 2 pods of cardamom in a mortar and pestle. Add the freshly ground cardamon to the flour mixture. Bake in a 13 inch by 9-inch rectangular pan. Soak with Tres Leches, chill, and serve to finish off a spicy curry feast.

Boozy Tres Leches: Add 1 to 2 tablespoons of rum.

10

Compote

Every cake in this book works wonderfully with a spoonful of compote served on the side. I make a triple berry compote with fresh berries, but frozen ones work just as well. You can also use pitted cherries or strawberries. You may wish to infuse the compote with a few sprigs of herbs, rosewater, or pure vanilla extract. I even swirl leftovers into a bowl of Greek yogurt the following morning for breakfast.

Makes 1½ to 1¾ cups;
enough for 6 to 8 side servings
Preparation: 15 minutes

1⅓ cups (185g) blueberries
1⅓ cups (175g) raspberries
1⅓ cups (145g) blackberries
2 tablespoons freshly squeezed lemon or orange juice
1 tablespoon freshly grated lemon or orange zest (optional)
1 to 2 tablespoon granulated sugar, pure Grade A maple syrup, or honey

Place the berries, juice, and zest in a heavy saucepan and gently cook on low heat until they swell and burst. Don't stir the berries too much, as you want them to keep their shape. Continue simmering for 10 to 15 minutes. Remove from the heat. Taste the compote and add the sweetener of choice as needed. Serve warm or chilled.

VARIATION

Berry Vanilla Compote: Add 1 teaspoon of pure vanilla extract while the compote is cooling.

TIP: If the Compote becomes too thick and doesn't have enough juice, just add a tablespoon or two of water.

Raspberry Curd

I guarantee that you'll be returning to the fridge throughout the day for a cheeky spoonful of this curd. Slather it on a slice of cake or gift a jar to a friend; either way, you'll be happy this recipe makes a little extra. Like the Caramel Sauce (page 92), when making curd, measure everything beforehand and have it at the ready. Using a double boiler is an insurance policy to prevent scrambling the eggs, and continual whisking is a must.

Makes 2¼ cups; enough for 8 to 10 side servings
Preparation: 20 minutes

1⅓ cups (175g) raspberries
5 eggs, at room temperature
¾ cup (150g) granulated sugar
⅛ teaspoon salt
Finely grated zest of 1 lemon
8 tablespoons (1 stick/115g) unsalted butter, at room temperature, cubed
½ cup (120ml) freshly squeezed lemon juice, strained

In the bottom of a double boiler, bring an inch of water to a gentle simmer on medium heat.

Place the raspberries in a ziplock bag or small bowl and crush them.

Whisk together the eggs, sugar, salt, and lemon zest in the top of a double boiler and then place on top of the simmering water. Make sure the bottom of the bowl doesn't touch the water. Continue whisking until the sugar has dissolved.

Add the butter, a cube at a time, making sure that each piece melts before another is added. The mixture will begin to thicken like a custard.

Finally, add the lemon juice and crushed raspberries and continue whisking until the curd thickens again. This process takes approximately 10 minutes or until a candy thermometer reads 165°F.

Strain the curd through a sieve. Cover the surface of the curd with a film of plastic wrap to stop a skin from forming. Store any extra curd in sealed sterilized jars. Keep in fridge.

VARIATIONS

Lemon and Lime Curd: Omit the raspberries. Replace ¼ cup (60ml) of the lemon juice with ¼ cup (60ml) of lime juice, strained.

Lemon and Passion Fruit Curd: Omit the raspberries. Replace ¼ cup (60ml) of the lemon juice with ¼ cup (60ml) of passion fruit juice. I like the crunch of the seeds, so I keep them, but you can strain the juice if you prefer.

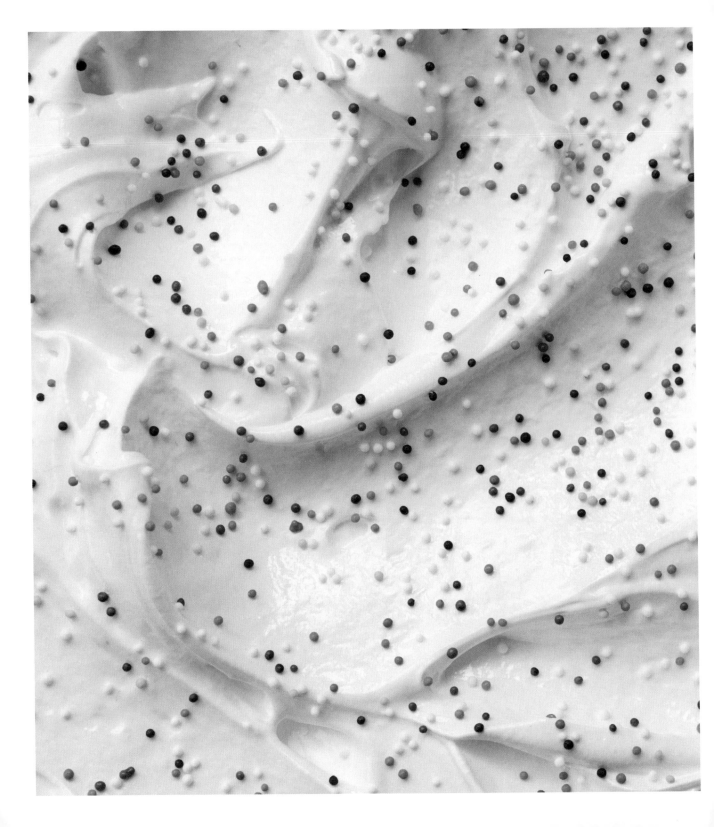

Silky Marshmallow Icing

**Makes 3 cups; enough for one
8- or 9-inch round cake
Preparation: 15 minutes**

2½ tablespoons water

2 large egg whites, at room
temperature

1 cup (200g) granulated sugar

¼ teaspoon cream of tartar

¼ teaspoon salt

1 teaspoon pure vanilla extract

Sweet. Soft. Childlike. Heaven. Every time I make this decadently sweet icing that kids and adults with a sweet tooth love, I just want to dive right into the bowl of white, silky, marshmallowy meringue. Don't be intimidated and think this will be too much work; it's really easy and doesn't take long. Simply throw all the ingredients in your mixing bowl over a double boiler, dissolve the sugar, heat the mixture, and then whisk as you would if you were making meringue.

Fill a medium saucepan with about 1½ inches of water, bring to a boil, and then lower the heat to maintain a gentle simmer.

Place the water, egg whites, sugar, cream of tartar, salt, and vanilla in a metal mixing bowl. (Use the mixing bowl of a stand mixer if you have one.) Place the bowl on top of the saucepan. Make sure the bottom of the bowl doesn't touch the water.

Whisk the mixture constantly for 4 minutes or until it reaches a temperature between 160° and 165°F if using a candy thermometer. The sugar will have dissolved, and the mixture will be opaque, bubbly, and very warm to the touch.

Carefully transfer the hot bowl to the electric mixer. Using a whisk attachment, beat the mixture on high speed for 4 minutes or until it's white and fluffy with stand-up peaks.

VARIATIONS

Vanilla Silky Marshmallow Icing: Rub the seeds from ½ of a vanilla bean into the sugar. Then add the sugar to the bowl along with the remaining ingredients.

Toasted Silky Marshmallow Icing: After decorating your cake, toast the Silky Marshmallow Icing to give it a lovely golden color. Use a cooking torch, or alternatively, place the decorated cake under a broiler. Watch it like a hawk because it can burn quickly; it only takes a minute or two.

Colored Silky Marshmallow Icing: At the very end of beating, add food coloring with a toothpick a little at a time, until you get your desired color. Remember: You can always add more but you can't take out extra.

Chocolate Swiss Meringue Buttercream

Caren Tommasone is the pastry chef at a fantastic catering company in my neighborhood. She is a creative baker who effortlessly produces the most beautiful cakes for large and small affairs on a daily basis. One day we were debating which topping was the most luxurious for decorative cakes. Swiss Meringue was where we landed. It lives between a meringue and buttercream, but we both find it much silkier and not as sweet as buttercream. It's the chocolate mousse of icing. Use an offset spatula to create drama by crafting peaks and valleys or swirls on top of the cake. The steps are the same as making the Silky Marshmallow Icing (page 87), except you add softened butter gradually to the beaten meringue and then any flavoring or coloring.

**Makes approximately 2½ cups; enough for one 10-inch round cake or 18 cupcakes
Preparation: 15 to 20 minutes.**

16 tablespoons (2 sticks/225g) unsalted butter, softened

3 egg whites, at room temperature

1 cup (200g) granulated sugar

¼ teaspoon cream of tartar

¼ teaspoon salt

½ teaspoon pure vanilla extract

2 tablespoons unsweetened Dutch-processed cocoa, sifted

Cut the butter into tablespoons.

Fill a medium saucepan with about 1½ inches of water, bring to a boil, then lower the heat to maintain a gentle simmer.

Place the egg whites, sugar, cream of tartar, and salt in the metal mixing bowl. (Use the mixing bowl of a stand mixer if you have one.) Place the bowl on top of the saucepan. Make sure the bottom of the bowl doesn't touch the water.

Whisk the mixture constantly for 4 minutes or until it reaches a temperature between 160° and 165°F if using a candy thermometer. The sugar will have dissolved, and the mixture will be opaque, bubbly, and very warm to the touch.

Carefully transfer the hot bowl to the electric mixer. Using a whisk attachment, beat the mixture on high speed for 4 minutes or until it's white and fluffy with stand-up peaks and more importantly, until the mixing bowl is no longer warm to the touch.

With the mixer still running, add the butter a tablespoon at a time. This helps keep the temperature stable. Scrape down the sides with a spatula.

Beat in the vanilla and the cocoa, until fully incorporated.

CAREN'S TIP: If the mixture looks too soupy, the ingredients are too hot. To remedy, put the mixing bowl back in the fridge to cool the ingredients before rebeating. If the mixture looks dense or curdled, the ingredients are too cold. Put the bowl back on the water bath until it starts to melt around the edges. Alternatively, and amazingly, if you continue to beat, it will come back together. It can also be frozen in an airtight container. To reuse, take the meringue out of the freezer to let it come to room temperature; rebeat it in the mixer until smooth.

VARIATIONS

Vanilla Bean Buttercream Meringue: Omit the chocolate. Rub the seeds from ½ of a vanilla bean into the sugar. Then add the sugar to the bowl along with the remaining ingredients.

Colored Buttercream Meringue: Got a kid's party? At the very end of beating, add food coloring with a toothpick a little at a time, until you get your desired color. Remember: You can always add more but you can't take out extra.

Crème Anglaise

America is all about à la mode, but I'm determined to bring custard into more homes in the United States, and the crème de la crème of custard is crème anglaise. It's a nice change from the usual cake toppings and great to accompany cake as a dessert at a dinner party. It's comforting but at the same time luxurious poured warm or cold over cake. It's better to have the crème anglaise runny than overcooked and cloudy. Adding cornstarch helps protect the eggs from overcooking and helps thicken the custard.

Makes approximately 1¾ cups; enough for 6 to 8 servings
Preparation: 15 minutes

1¾ cups (420ml) whole milk
4 egg yolks
⅓ cup (65g) granulated sugar
2 teaspoons cornstarch
1 teaspoon pure vanilla extract

In a heavy saucepan over low heat, gently heat the milk until little bubbles start to appear around the edge of the pan; do not boil.

Meanwhile, in a medium bowl, whisk the egg yolks, sugar, and cornstarch for a couple of minutes, until pale in color.

Take the milk off the heat and slowly pour it onto the egg and sugar mixture, whisking constantly. Return all of the mixture to the saucepan. On low heat, continuously stir the custard using a wooden spoon. Slowly bring the custard's temperature up to between 175° and 180°F. This should take approximately 8 minutes. When cooked, crème anglaise will look silky—not thick. The custard should coat the spoon, and if you run your finger over the back of it, a line should remain.

Remove from the heat immediately so it doesn't continue to cook and pour the custard through a fine mesh strainer.

Whisk in the vanilla.

VARIATIONS

Vanilla Bean Anglaise: Infuse the milk as it's warming with 1 vanilla bean, split lengthwise. Before adding the milk to the eggs, retrieve the vanilla bean and scrape out the seeds. Add them back to the milk and continue to cook as directed.

Chocolate Anglaise: Add ¼ cup (40g) of semisweet chocolate chips along with the vanilla, and whisk until the chocolate melts.

Boozy Anglaise: Add 1 tablespoon of liqueur such as Grand Marnier or Amaretto.

Caramel Sauce

You'll probably burn your first batch of this sauce and undercook the second, but after that, it will be game on. Through experience, you will recognize when the bulk of the water has evaporated, and the sugar has cooked to a deep golden, amber color. Watch carefully in the final moments so you don't burn it. When in doubt, pull the ripcord sooner rather than later because it can happen quickly. Remove the saucepan from the heat, add the butter, and whisk in the cream. This skill will open up a new door into your dessert world. The sauce is delicious served warm over the Chocolatey Chocolate Cake (page 22) with a scoop of ice cream and a sprinkling of sea salt. (See also the Sleepover Cake on page 150.) I gave a jar of this sauce to a friend whose husband called it crack cocaine. Once you know it's in the fridge, you won't be able to stop going back for more. Caramel can be made in advance, and I recommend doing this if you have friends coming.

Makes 1¼ cups: enough for 6 or 7 servings
Preparation: 15 minutes

1 cup (200g) granulated sugar
½ cup (120ml) water
7 tablespoons (100g) unsalted butter, diced
½ cup (120ml) heavy cream
½ teaspoon pure vanilla extract
½ teaspoon salt

Have a whisk, the measured ingredients, a medium heavy saucepan, and a timer ready. Make sure the saucepan is light in color; otherwise, it will be difficult to see the color of the caramel as it's cooking.

Add the sugar and water to the saucepan.

Over medium heat, begin to cook the sugar mix. Do not stir; swirl the pan if you see dry sugar spots or if the sugar is cooking unevenly. Use a wet pastry brush and extra water to paint off any sugar that crystallizes on the side of the pan. Continue to cook the bubbly sugar mix until it's a rich amber color. This will take anywhere from 12 to 15 minutes. Watch the pan really carefully in the final minutes, since it's a fine line between perfect and burnt. When ready, remove the pan from the heat and add the butter, whisking until it's completely melted. It may splatter a little. Add the cream and continue whisking until incorporated. Let the mixture cool slightly before adding the vanilla and the salt.

30

Cake-Worthy Moments

CELEBRATING WITH CAKE

Here are thirty cake designs and flavor combinations
that hopefully inspire you to begin experimenting
with the 10 cake and 15 cake topping recipes. I've
made suggestions for when or why they might be
appreciated in life, but of course it's not gospel. I layer,
slice, dice, and cut cake into shapes. They are baked
in all sorts of pans and vessels, from the standards to
ramekins, skillets, and specialty pans. Dinner parties,
tournaments, fund-raisers, roadtrips, sleepovers, and,
of course, birthdays are all covered here.

TLC Cakes

Tender. Loving. Care. This kind trio of words is made kinder when put into action and cake. Here are some cakes you might like to bake for yourself or deliver to others to let them know they are loved, welcomed, supported, rewarded, congratulated, or valued. No big bells and whistles in this lineup, just delicious, yummy cake with contrasting textures and tastes that will make people happy. The unexpected crunch of sea salt on top of the silky sweet Chocolate Swiss Meringue Buttercream (page 88) on the Bribery Cake (page 101) would make anyone's day. The heavenly moment when you scoop a spoonful of the Lazy Lamington cake (page 102) and feel the toasted coconut and shaved chocolate fall into the pillows of whipped cream is the equivalent of a hug. And what's not to love about a slice of the Versatile Coconut Cake (page 42) pan-fried in butter?

① A Self-Care Cake

This cake is for those times in life when you're not firing on all cylinders. For comfort, my dad used to make my brother and me a mug of warm milk, adding a few teaspoons of honey for a sweet, nurturing drink, so this combination of flavors always lifts my spirits. After the cake is baked, sit yourself down, cut a slice while it's still slightly warm, and drizzle with a little honey or add a dollop of Honey Whipped Cream. In fact, cut as many slices as you bloody well like. If polishing off two 9-inch cakes is too much self-care, halve the recipe or freeze one for another S.O.S. day.

Makes two 9-inch round cakes

Milk and Honey Cake (page 34)
Honey Whipped Cream (page 75), optional

Confectioners' sugar, for dusting
Honey, for drizzling

Preheat the oven to 350°F. Prepare pans. Make the batter for the Milk and Honey Cake according to directions. Bake in the center of the oven for 30 to 35 minutes or until a wooden skewer inserted in the center comes out clean, and the cake bounces back when lightly pressed. Cool the cakes on a wire rack. Dust with the confectioners' sugar and serve. If you're feeling impatient and want to enjoy the cake warm, drizzle a slice with honey or add a dollop of Honey Whipped Cream.

Bribery Cake

A not-too-sweet chocolate cake, topped with silky Chocolate Swiss Meringue Buttercream, sprinkled with a little sea salt crunch: This is the cake you bake to help you or a loved one get across the finish line.

Makes one 9-inch square cake or approximately 24 cupcakes

Chocolatey Chocolate Cake (page 22)

Chocolate Swiss Meringue Buttercream (page 88)

Maldon sea salt (optional)

Preheat the oven to 350°F. Prepare pan. If you are making cupcakes, line the cupcake pans with foil paper liners (foil liners are sturdier, as this batter is runny); don't fill liners more than halfway. Make the batter for the Chocolatey Chocolate Cake according to directions. Bake a 9-inch square cake for 35 to 40 minutes and cupcakes for 20 to 25 minutes, or until a wooden skewer inserted in the center comes out clean, and the cake bounces back when lightly pressed.

While the cake or cupcakes are baking, make the Chocolate Swiss Meringue Buttercream according to directions.

Cool cake on a wire rack. Ice the top of the cake or the tops of the cupcakes with the buttercream. Sprinkle with sea salt.

Lazy Lamington

Homesickness always seems to creep up unannounced. I've come up with some nifty ways to quell the longing: I Google images of beaches I grew up on, sit and watch Australian football games with my husband that I'd normally have zero interest in, or bake cakes that remind me of home. For those of you unfamiliar with the iconic Australian lamington, or lammo as it's often called, it's a sponge cake cut into individual square portions, dipped in a runny chocolate icing that soaks into the sponge, and then rolled in shredded coconut. A top-notch lamington will have jam and cream in the middle. Lamingtons are a messy affair that take time to bake, which is why most Australians buy them at local bakeries or at fund-raisers. One afternoon, I was craving a lamington but was too lazy to make the real thing; that's when I came up with the Lazy Lamington. It has all the key flavors: coconut, berries, chocolate, and cream, but I've nixed the sponge cake. The Lazy Lamington can be baked in most of the pans that I recommend for the Versatile Coconut Cake (except for the Bundt). It's a one-pan lamington that's meant to be shared with friends and multiple spoons.

Makes one 10½ by 7½-inch cake, or one 8-inch round cake

Versatile Coconut Cake (page 42)
Vanilla Whipped Cream (page 75)

1⅓ cups (170g) raspberries
¾ cup (35g) unsweetened coconut flakes, toasted
½ cup (50g) semisweet chocolate, shaved

Preheat the oven to 350°F. Grease a 10½ by 7½-inch ceramic dish with butter. (There's no need to use parchment paper if you're going to serve straight from dish.) Make the batter for the Versatile Coconut Cake according to directions. Cut the raspberries in half and fold them gently into the batter. Bake for approximately 30 minutes or until a wooden skewer inserted in the center comes out clean, and the cake bounces back when lightly pressed. Keep the cake in the dish and cool completely on a wire rack.

Make the Vanilla Whipped Cream. Using a spoon, dollop the cream on top of the cake. Don't spread it out; you want to keep the volume in the cream. Finally, sprinkle the toasted coconut and chocolate shavings on top.

A Golden Buttery Treat

If you have the house to yourself and no one can witness this indulgence, go for it—it's the perfect pick-me-up. Pan-frying a slice of cake, no matter what flavor, adds a delicious nutty flavor similar to browned butter and creates a scrumptious, crisp exterior. This is also a clever way to revive cake that's a few days old. For best results, use a loaf cake without any icing. Fry one slice at a time, being careful not to burn the butter. This buttery treat is ideal for a late breakfast or even for supper with a scoop of ice cream.

Makes 1 slice

1 slice Versatile Coconut Cake
(page 42)

**2 tablespoons unsalted butter,
at room temperature, per slice**

Cut a slice of cake about an inch thick. In a small heavy frying pan on low heat, melt the butter until it begins to bubble and brown. Swirl the butter around the pan, then add the slice of cake. Gently cook one side until it's golden brown, then flip it. This takes about a minute for each side. Serve warm.

Comfort Cakes

I remember standing in the narrow galley kitchen of our one-bedroom Manhattan apartment the week after having given birth to our daughter Opal and having an overwhelming craving for cake. In retrospect, I'm not sure how I juggled baking a cake while holding a newborn, but I was obviously desperate for sweet comfort myself. Those early weeks and months with a new baby are such a blur—there's no time or energy for cooking, and yet never before have you needed the fuel the way you do now. If you take a cake to a friend who has just had a baby, she'll love you forever. Adding a jar of Caramel Sauce (page 92) or Raspberry Curd (page 84) that she can sneak a spoonful of during those sleepless nights is not a bad idea either.

Makes one 8 by 3-inch Bundt cake

Very Vanilla Cake (page 26) or Versatile Coconut Cake (page 42)
Nana's Simple Glaze (page 70)

Comfort Cake for a New Parent

Preheat the oven to 350°F. Grease an 8 by 3-inch Bundt pan generously with butter and lightly dust with flour, shaking off any excess. Make the batter for the Very Vanilla Cake or the Versatile Coconut Cake according to the directions. Bake for approximately 30 minutes or until a wooden skewer inserted in the Bundt comes out clean, and it bounces back when lightly pressed. Cool the cake on a wire rack. Bundle it up and deliver along with a jar of glaze, curd, or sauce.

Makes approximately 24 madeleines

Chocolate Madeleines (page 53)

2 tablespoons confectioners' sugar
1 tablespoon unsweetened Dutch-processed cocoa powder

Comfort Cake for a Friend in Need

Preheat the oven to 350°F. Prepare the madeleine pans for Chocolate Madeleines. Make the batter for the Chocolate Madeleines according to directions. Bake for approximately 8 to 10 minutes or until the edges have pulled away slightly from the shell. Cool on a wire rack.

Mix the confectioners' sugar and cocoa together in a small bowl and use a sifter or fine tea strainer to dust the tops of the madeleines.

All Day, Everyday Cakes

Even when in high rotation, these cakes never get old. Like good friendships, they're easy and familiar, and that's why they're beloved. The Lovely Lemon Yogurt Cake (page 46) baked as a loaf is timeless and sublime. Very Vanilla Cupcakes (page 29) are mandatory. Tangy Olive Oil Cake (page 38) will always be welcome no matter the occasion, and the individual Meringues (page 58) are a must.

Loaf on the Go

This is the perfect cake for a road trip, picnic, or any time you're on the go. It's super easy to transport and is wonderful with a spoonful of Lemon and Lime Curd. Don't forget to pack a knife and some salty pistachios along with the cake and curd.

Makes one 9 by 5-inch loaf cake

- -

Lovely Lemon Yogurt Cake
(page 46)
Lemon and Lime Curd (page 84)

Handful of shelled salted pistachios
(optional)

Preheat the oven to 350°F. Prepare loaf pan. Make the batter for the Lovely Lemon Yogurt Cake according to directions. Bake in the center of the oven for 50 to 55 minutes or until a wooden skewer inserted in the center comes out clean, and the cake bounces back when lightly pressed.

While the loaf is baking, make the Lemon and Lime Curd according to the directions. Spoon the curd into a transportable container. Serve the cake with the curd and sprinkle with pistachios.

⑦ "Have Another Cup of Tea" Cupcakes

Whatever happened to dropping in on someone unannounced? When I was young, we would often drop in at our aunt and uncle's house, where Mum would catch up with my aunt, and my brother and I would run around with our cousins, climbing trees and playing cops and robbers. We always had so much fun that we never wanted to leave. When we sensed that things were wrapping up, my cousins and I would head into the kitchen and try to convince our mothers to "have another cup of tea!"

These cupcakes are perfect for impromptu visits such as those, since they're quick to bang out and best when really fresh. In less than an hour, you'll have 12 fluffy cupcakes topped with a generous smear of Mascarpone Easy Creamy Icing. If the season's right, decorate them with flowering herbs, or you can always add some sprinkles or raspberries. With these cupcakes, I hereby declare visiting season open every day.

Makes approximately 12 cupcakes

Very Vanilla Cake (page 26)
Mascarpone Easy Creamy Icing (page 72)

Preheat the oven to 350°F. Line the cupcake pan with paper liners. Make the batter for the Very Vanilla Cake according to the directions. Bake for 15 to 20 minutes or until the cupcakes have colored slightly and spring back when gently pressed in the center. Cool the cupcakes completely on a wire rack. Make the Mascarpone Easy Creamy Icing. Ice the cupcakes. Decorate or just eat as is.

Weekday or Weekend Meringues

What's not to love about breaking into a crisp Vanilla and Chocolate Swirl Meringue with a gooey center, topped with the triple-berry compote and Vanilla Whipped Cream? Absolutely nothing. That's not to mention how ridiculously dreamy the color palate is. When I just want dessert to be a no-brainer, I make individual meringues. Everyone loves them, everything can be prepped before friends arrive, and they're evergreen. Check, check, check.

Makes 8 to 10 individual meringues

Vanilla and Chocolate Swirl Meringue (page 61)
Compote (page 83)
Vanilla Whipped Cream (page 75)

Preheat the oven to 300°F. Make the batter for the individual Vanilla and Chocolate Swirl Meringues according to directions. Make sure to turn the oven temperature down to 250°F before putting the individual meringues in the oven. Bake for approximately 40 minutes or until crisp on the outside. Check on the meringues after the first 10 minutes to make sure they're not browning too much. If they are, turn the oven down a little bit more.

After the meringues have baked, turn off the oven. Leave the meringues in the oven where it's dry and free from moisture until it's time to serve. Make Compote and Vanilla Whipped Cream. Plate the meringues, spoon on the Compote, and then put a dollop of Vanilla Whipped Cream on top.

A Dining-In Cake

This cake is high-end simplicity—a perfect year-round dessert to serve when friends are coming or the family needs a treat. One evening at ABC Cocina, one of Jean-Georges Vongerichten's New York restaurants, I had a sublime, elegantly plated slice of tres leches cake for dessert. I came home and made my own chocolate version using the Chocolatey Chocolate Cake. It's so easy and can be made ahead of time. You simply bake a sheet cake in the morning, poke and soak the cake with Tres Leches, and refrigerate. To plate, I cut the cake into fingers, then loosely dollop Condensed Milk Whipped Cream along each slice and generousy sprinkle with chocolate shavings.

Makes one 13 by 9-inch sheet cake; individual servings in ramekins work well, too

Chocolatey Chocolate Cake
(page 22)
Tres Leches (page 81)
Condensed Milk Whipped Cream
(page 75)

½ cup (55g) semisweet chocolate
shavings (optional)

Preheat the oven to 350°F. Grease pan with butter, but don't line the pan with parchment paper because it will prevent the cake from soaking up the Tres Leches. Make the batter for the Chocolatey Chocolate Cake according to directions. Bake for 25 to 30 minutes or until a wooden skewer inserted in the center comes out clean, and the cake bounces back when lightly pressed.

While the cake is baking, make the Tres Leches.

Cool cake in the pan. Use a skewer to poke small holes through the cake, about an inch apart. Slowly spoon the Tres Leches over the top of the cake, giving it time to soak in. Once the liquid is absorbed, repeat until all the Tres Leches is used. (Toward the end, the Tres Leches will pool at the edges, but don't worry; it will be absorbed while in the fridge.) Cover the cake with plastic wrap and refrigerate overnight or for at least 5 to 6 hours. (If you're really pressed for time, a couple of hours will also work.)

Before serving, make the Condensed Milk Whipped Cream (double the recipe if you would like extra whipped cream). If you want to be casual, just smother the cake with the cream, sprinkle the chocolate shavings on top, and serve from the pan. If you want more elegant slices, trim the perimeter of the cake using a large, sharp knife. Then cut the cake into finger slices, wiping the knife clean between each slice. Dollop whipped cream across each slice and then sprinkle with chocolate shavings.

A Cake by Day and by Night

Individual servings of the Tangy Olive Oil Cake are the little black dresses of cakes. They're perfect to have in your repertoire, since they will work for both day and night.

Makes approximately 24 standard or fluted cupcakes

Tangy Olive Oil Cake (page 38)
Nana's Simple Glaze (page 70)

Edible flowers (optional)

Dressed for the Day

Preheat the oven to 350°F. If you are using individual fluted cupcake pans, grease generously with butter, using your fingers to get into all the grooves, and then lightly dust with flour, shaking off any excess. Alternatively, line standard cupcake pans with paper liners. Make the batter for the Tangy Olive Oil Cake according to directions. Fill each vessel two thirds full. Bake for 17 to 20 minutes or until the cupcakes have slightly colored and spring back when gently pressed in the center. Cool cupcakes on a wire rack. Make Nana's Simple Glaze. Spoon glaze over cupcakes and add edible flowers on top.

Makes 12 individual Bundt cakes

Tangy Olive Oil Cake (page 38)
Boozy Crème Anglaise (page 91)

½ cup (55g) sliced almonds, toasted (optional)

Dressed for the Night

Preheat the oven to 350°F. Grease the cavities of the Bundt pans generously with butter, using your fingers to get into all the grooves, then lightly dust with flour, shaking off any excess. Make the batter for the Tangy Olive Oil Cake according to directions. Fill each Bundt cavity two thirds full. Bake for 20 to 25 minutes or until a wooden skewer inserted into the Bundts comes out clean and bounces back when lightly pressed. Cool the cakes on a wire rack.

Meanwhile, make the Boozy Anglaise. (It can be served hot or cold.) Plate the individual Bundts and pour on the Crème Anglaise just before serving. Top with toasted almonds, if desired.

A Cake for the Working Week

Gear up for the week by baking this cake on a Sunday afternoon. You might want to play Dolly Parton's "Nine to Five" while you do. The syrup keeps this homey citrus cake moist for days, so if it manages to last until Wednesday, it will still be delicious. Alternatively, take this all-rounder to work to celebrate a colleague's birthday or farewell.

Makes one 9-inch round cake

Poppy Seed Yogurt Cake (page 49)
Citrus Syrup (page 78)

Preheat the oven to 350°F. Prepare pan. Make the batter for the Poppy Seed Yogurt Cake according to directions. Bake for 40 to 45 minutes or until a wooden skewer inserted in the center comes out clean, and the cake bounces back when lightly pressed. While the cake is baking, make the Citrus Syrup according to directions. Keep the syrup runny so it penetrates the cake. Place cake on a wire rack that sits over a dinner plate to catch any drips when you add the syrup to the cake. Poke holes about an inch apart in the top of the cake with a skewer and slowly spoon the syrup over the top of the cake, gradually letting it soak in.

Pattern Playground Cakes

Cake has a way of transporting you back to childhood. I'm sure that's why we enjoy eating it so much as adults. Sometimes we grown-ups can lose the ability to get ridiculously excited. I'm reminded of this when I find my daughter Opal's lists and diagrams that map out her party plans months in advance of her birthday. It takes me back to standing over my brother's shoulder watching him make his birthday cake selection from the *Australian Women's Weekly Children's Birthday Cake Book* every October. I'd live vicariously through him, waiting with bated breath to see what he'd choose. I'd then sit down and begin bookmarking my picks, even though my birthday wasn't until February.

For birthdays in my household, each kid gets to choose his or her cake. I'll shop, we bake, and my husband helps sculpt and decorate the more elaborate cakes. It's a family affair to get ready for the party. Some years a simple, tasty cake that you can whack a few candles on like Little Treasures (page 127) or Big Ted's Birthday Cake (page 128) will do the trick. Other times, a cake that becomes a family legend is called for, like the Winter Wonderland Cake (page 135). At the party, the grown-ups can always drink; and the cake is the star.

Polka Dot Tea Party Mini Cupcakes

Who knew you could draw on a cake? I discovered you could one afternoon when I was playing around with edible markers, drawing simple, repeat patterns like polka dots and small flowers on fondant. When the kids and my goddaughter, Olivia, saw me doing this, they were beside themselves. I set each of them up with their own ball of fondant, a rolling pin, a cookie cutter, and edible markers, and they unleashed their inner Picassos and Kahlos. This is a fun activity to do at a kid's birthday party, and the bite-size cupcakes enable kids to eat a couple of their designs—or maybe twenty if left unsupervised. Make sure you read Tips for Working with Fondant on page 67 before you begin.

Makes approximately 45 mini cupcakes

Very Vanilla Cake (page 26)
Easy Creamy Icing (page 72)

Cornstarch or confectioners' sugar, for dusting surface

1 pound (450g) white vanilla fondant, such as Satin Ice or Wilton

Edible markers, such as AmeriColor Gourmet Writer Food Decorating Pens

To make the cupcakes: Preheat the oven to 350°F. Line the mini cupcake pans with paper liners. Make the batter for the Very Vanilla Cake according to directions. Bake for 12 to 14 minutes, or until the cupcakes have slightly colored and spring back when lightly pressed in the center. The mini cupcakes can easily overcook and become dry, so keep an eye on them. Note that if you're using foil cupcake liners, the bottoms of the cupcakes will cook faster. Depending on the size of your oven, you may have to bake these in batches. Cool cupcakes completely on wire rack.

To make the fondant disks: While the cupcakes are cooling, line a large baking tray with parchment paper. Dust a little cornstarch or confectioners' sugar onto a clean, dry nonstick surface such as marble. Fondant is like working with Play-Doh. Work the fondant, rolling it between your hands, to soften. Divide the fondant into two balls; it's easier to work with in smaller batches. Cover the unused fondant well with plastic wrap to stop it from drying out. Flatten the other ball between your palms and then use a rolling pin to roll it out. Lift and rotate the disk a few times so that it doesn't stick to the surface. Don't flip it. You want the fondant smooth, free from cracks, and about ⅛ to ¼ inch thick. If it's too thin, it will lose its shape when you try to lift it off the surface; if it's too thick, it will dominate the flavor of the cupcake. Use a 1½-inch round cookie cutter or a thin-rimmed glass to cut out the disks. Peel away any excess fondant around the disks. The fondant will be soft, so

be careful not to dent the disks: gently place an offset spatula or sharp knife underneath the disk, pressing into the surface and shimmying underneath the disk until it's released. Set the disk aside on parchment paper. Repeat this process until all of the disks have been prepared. Of course, kids will have a more haphazard approach, and that's just dandy.

To make the icing and to decorate: Make the Easy Creamy Icing. Ice the cupcakes. Have the kids draw on the disks with the edible markers. Finally, place the doodled disks on top of the iced cupcakes.

13 Little Treasures Cake

Have you noticed how obsessed little kids are with teeny, tiny things? I'm sure I am not alone in having a graveyard full of small, unidentified toys. This cake is an edible version inspired by those little treasures. In Williamsburg, Brooklyn, there's a bakery, Sweethaus, that sells cakes and candies. If this is the cake of choice for someone's birthday, then we head to Sweethaus, where the kids choose old-school candies to bring home and decorate the top of this cake. Seeing them make their selections takes me back to spending my own twenty-five-cent pocket money on mixed lollies. On the morning of the party, I'll make the Very Vanilla Cake, ice it, and then let the kids decorate it before the icing sets.

Makes one 8-inch round cake

Very Vanilla Cake (page 26)
Easy Creamy Icing (page 72)

Food coloring (optional)
Assorted candies

Preheat the oven to 350°F. Prepare pan. Make the batter for the Very Vanilla Cake according to directions. Bake for 35 to 40 minutes or until a wooden skewer inserted in the center comes out clean, and the cake bounces back when lightly pressed. Cool the cake on a wire rack.

Make the Easy Creamy Icing. Using a toothpick, sparingly tint the icing with food coloring. Ice the cake. Before the icing sets, get the birthday boy or girl to decorate the cake with the candies.

Big Ted's Birthday Cake

This is just the thing for those long, rainy days when you're stuck inside with a small child and you somehow have to fill the hours. Grab a cardboard box, some pillows, some toys, and a few of their beloved stuffed animals to make a party. Bake the Very Vanilla Cake, drizzle it with Citrus Glaze until it starts to cling to the sides of the cake, light a candle, and sing "Happy Birthday" to Big Ted.

Makes one 6 by 3-inch round cake

Very Vanilla Cake (page 26)
Citrus Glaze (page 70)

Preheat the oven to 350°F. Prepare pan. Make the batter for the Very Vanilla Cake according to directions. Bake for 50 to 55 minutes or until a wooden skewer inserted in the center comes out clean, and the cake bounces back when lightly pressed. Cover the top of the cake with aluminum foil after 30 minutes so the cake doesn't take on too much color. Cool the cake on a wire rack.

Make the Citrus Glaze. You want the glaze to be a consistency that clings to the cake. Evenly pour just enough glaze on top of the center of the cake, until it starts to drip slightly down the sides of the cake.

Over the Moon Cake

This is the cake to make when everyone is over the moon for having reached another milestone. Kids will enjoy making this cake alongside you, and they will love nibbling on the morsels even more. The cake is decadent served slightly warm, but the stars are easier to cut out, and they hold their shapes better, when the cake has had time to rest. If you don't have a star cookie cutter, use a sharp knife to cut out the stars and the moon. (And to be honest, hearts, diamonds, or even circles are just as cute.) If making the Caramel Sauce feels like too much work, try serving the cake with Compote (page 83) or just the Vanilla Whipped Cream. Don't chase perfection with this cake; instead, enjoy licking your fingers.

Makes two 8-inch round cakes

Milk and Honey Cake (page 34)
Vanilla Whipped Cream (page 75)
Caramel Sauce (page 92)

Preheat the oven to 350°F. Prepare pans. Make the batter for the Milk and Honey Cake according to directions. Bake side by side on the same oven rack for 35 to 38 minutes or until a wooden skewer inserted in the center comes out clean, and the cake bounces back when lightly pressed. Cool the cakes completely on a wire rack.

While the cakes are cooling, make the Caramel Sauce and Vanilla Whipped Cream. Use a large sharp knife to cut both cakes horizontally through the middle. Lay the four pieces of cake on a clean, dry, hard surface. Cut a crescent moon shape out and with the remaining cake, use a star cookie cutter to cut out stars. Use a small sharp knife to cut around the edges of the cookie cutter to help get clean lines around the stars. Gently encourage the cake out of the cookie cutter by pushing it with your finger.

Line a large chopping board or tray with parchment paper, and lay out the stars and moon. Serve with caramel sauce and cream.

Back-to-School Cake

I get tired of buying the supposedly healthy snack foods available for kids these days. I'd rather send my kids off to school with a treat I've baked, knowing what's gone into it. I definitely don't bake every week, but when I do, it makes the daily routine a little sweeter. In an hour on a lazy Sunday afternoon, I know that I can bake enough cake for the week. The Lovely Lemon Yogurt Cake (page 46) with Citrus Syrup (page 78), the Versatile Coconut Cake (page 42), and the Cinnamon Spice Cake (page 30) are also all great back-to-school candidates, since they will keep fresh for days.

Makes one 13 by 9-inch rectangular cake

Chocolatey Chocolate Cake (page 22)

Confectioners' sugar, for dusting

Preheat the oven to 350°F. Prepare pan. Make the batter for the Chocolatey Chocolate Cake according to directions. Bake for 25 to 30 minutes or until a wooden skewer inserted in the center comes out clean, and the cake bounces back when lightly pressed. Cool the cake completely on wire rack. Dust the top of the cake with confectioners' sugar and then place in an airtight container or in an old-timey tin if you want to get really nostalgic. Slice as needed throughout the week.

Winter Wonderland Cake

This off-piste pièce de résistance was a joyous team effort between my old friend Mikaela and me. We were sitting around one night brainstorming ideas for a cake that could be the ultimate homage to the *Australian Women's Weekly Children's Birthday Cake Book*. Mikaela and I grew up in Australia, and because we both found the wintry Northern Hemisphere imagery otherworldly and romantic, we decided to create a cake that was a snowy, winter wonderland.

I was charged with baking and making the majestic swirls of icing while Mikaela took the craft paper, string, skewers, and toothpicks home and created the epic chairlift. The vintage animals we found on Etsy, and I was told by the seller that delivery would be slow because they were "in hibernation." I'm really not sure who was more excited—the kids or us—when we started cake construction. This cake definitely takes a little longer, and you'll curse at me when one of the chairlifts falls into the icing, but the joy is found in the challenge of pulling it off.

The cake is essentially a blank canvas: a double recipe of Funfetti Very Vanilla Cake smothered in Silky Marshmallow Icing, so theoretically any theme could decorate it. If you don't own a 6 by 3-inch springform pan, use two 8-inch round pans and cut a smaller circle out of one cake so that you get the levels between layers.

Makes one 6 by 3-inch and one 8-inch round cake

Double batch of Funfetti Vanilla Cake (page 29)
Silky Marshmallow Icing (page 87)

Confectioners' sugar, for dusting

Preheat the oven to 350°F. Prepare one 6 by 3-inch springform pan and one 8-inch round pan. Double the recipe for the Funfetti Vanilla Cake and make the batter according to directions. Divide the batter between the pans. Place both cakes in the oven on the same shelf and bake for the suggested times (for the 8-inch pan: 35 to 40 minutes; for the 6 by 3-inch pan: 50 to 55 minutes). Take the 8-inch cake out when it's done. Take this opportunity to cover the remaining cake with a little aluminum foil to stop it from taking on too much color. Keep the 6 by 3-inch cake baking, until a wooden skewer inserted in the center comes out clean, and the cake bounces back when

continued

lightly pressed. Cool the cakes completely on a wire rack and remove them from the tins. If a dome has formed on the 6 by 3-inch cake, cut it off when it's cool, so the cake can sit flat.

Make the Silky Marshmallow Icing.

Layer the cakes on top of each other on a serving plate with the smaller cake on top and off to one side, not centered. Dust off any crumbs. Ice the cakes. To achieve drama with the icing, use an offset spatula or spoon and flick your wrist to make the peaks and swirls. Dust the trees with confectioners' sugar and place them on the cake. Position the other decorations, as desired.

Equipment to make the chairlift and decorate the cake:

Pencil

Craft paper, medium weight

X-Acto knife or small scissors

Natural fine baker's twine

3 wooden skewers

3 flat toothpicks

Miniature trees

Miniature winter animals

1. Using a pencil, draw four chairs on the craft paper. Cut out the chair shapes with an X-Acto knife or small scissors.

2. With an X-Acto knife or small scissors, poke a small hole in the vertical beam of each chair.

3. Cut, thread, and tie a small piece of twine through the hole of each chair.

4. To make the towers, use an X-Acto knife or small scissors to make a small slit in the top of each skewer and then wedge a toothpick at a right angle into each.

5. Place the skewers into the cake.

6. Cut two long pieces of twine. Loop and tie at each crossbar. Make sure the twine is not loose; otherwise, your chairs might fall into the icing. Cut off any excess twine.

7. Very, very gently tie the chairs onto the cable.

8. Position the trees and the animals.

9. HIGH FIVES ALL AROUND!

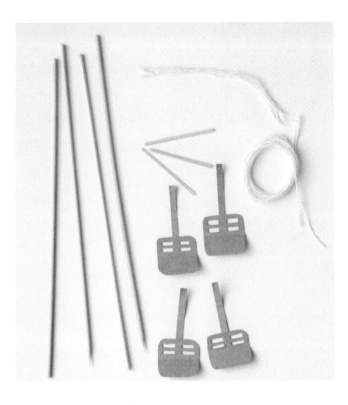

Growing Family and Friends Cakes

I come from a large extended family. Growing up, I loved staying at my aunt and uncle's home. The adults kept the household running, while my five cousins came and went throughout the day to and from sports, music lessons, and weekend jobs. I loved their open-door policy; pets meandered in and out, and everyone congregated somewhere between the fridge and the oven. There was security and love in every nook and cranny of that house.

I'm sure having that experience was why I wanted a large family of my own. I didn't quite get to five kids, but I am fortunate to be a stepmother to Dixie and Matilda and mother to Opal and Ned. In addition to the kiddos, I fill our Brooklyn brownstone with a never-ending rotation of visiting family and friends. My husband jokes that I'm afraid of being alone with him, but fortunately, I married an accommodating, generous, social man who is happy to share me.

The cakes in this section are inspired by my clan. They are cakes I bake for them and sometimes with them, for special occasions, celebrations, fund-raisers, sleepovers, tennis tournaments, and holiday festivities. Passion fruit and coconut brighten up the daytime cakes, while chocolate, hazelnut, and caramel make evenings that much better.

The Loveliest Layered Cake

Babies and exhausted parents don't need a big affair to celebrate the major milestone of a first birthday. And let's face it: when your child turns one, the cake is not for them; it's for you. You made it! You survived the insane first year. Using a 6 by 3-inch springform pan, the scale of this cake is so adorable; it's one of the pans I use most. If you don't own one, I really recommend making the investment. It bakes a petite cake, which can be layered if you wish and easily polished off in one sitting. Ice it with either the Passion Fruit Buttercream or the Blueberry Buttercream and then decorate it with edible flowers or flowering herbs.

PS: This cake could also remedy a wounded heart after the arrival of another sibling.

Makes one 6 by 3-inch layer cake

Very Vanilla Cake (page 26)
**Passion Fruit Buttercream or
Blueberry Buttercream** (page 73)

Edible flowers or flowering herbs
(optional)

Preheat the oven to 350°F. Prepare pan. Make the batter for the Very Vanilla Cake according to directions. Bake for 50 to 55 minutes or until a wooden skewer inserted in the center comes out clean, and the cake bounces back when lightly pressed. Cover the top of the cake with aluminum foil after 30 minutes so the cake doesn't take on too much color.

While the cake is baking, make the buttercream.

Cool the cake on a wire rack. If you want the top of the cake level, cut off the dome using a large sharp knife. Then cut the cake horizontally through the middle to create two layers. Ice the cake, being careful not to kick up too many crumbs. Decorate with edible flowers or flowering herbs, if desired, before the icing has set.

"How Did You Get So Big?" Cake

I can't believe how much my kids grow every year, and how quickly their birthdays roll around. Didn't I just bake them a birthday cake? That was a year ago? Are all those gray hairs mine? If you need to bake a kid's birthday kind of cake, this is it! The moist Chocolatey Chocolate Cake, topped with Silky Marshmallow Icing and a teeny, tiny pop of sprinkles tastes and feels like childhood. After Ned had this cake for his last birthday, I asked him what he wanted for his next year's cake. His answer? This one.

Makes one 10-inch round cake

Chocolatey Chocolate Cake
(page 22)
Silky Marshmallow Icing (page 87)

Rainbow nonpareil sprinkles
(optional)

Preheat the oven to 350°F. Prepare pan. Make the batter for the Chocolatey Chocolate Cake according to directions. Bake for approximately 50 minutes or until a wooden skewer inserted in the center comes out clean, and the cake bounces back when lightly pressed. Cool cake completely on wire rack.

While the cake is baking, make the Silky Marshmallow Icing.

Ice the cake using a spatula or a metal spoon to create peaks and valleys without kicking up dark crumbs. You'll have a little icing left over if you want to spread a layer across the middle of the cake. Add the rainbow nonpareil sprinkles, if desired.

Love, Set, Match Cake

Here, I'm marrying my two loves, tennis and cake. When I wasn't old enough to go to school, I used to tag along and watch my mum play tennis at the local courts with a few women from the neighborhood. It sounds posh, but it really wasn't. It was hot as hell and dusty. The ladies wore all whites and wielded wooden racquets, while I waited patiently for morning tea. After a long hiatus, I recently returned to the tennis court. It started with a game of doubles with friends—full of sweat and swearing. It was a ridiculous amount of fun. We've since made it an annual match, and the winners get to take home a trophy. One day I'll make it to Wimbledon, where strawberries and cream are de rigueur. By coincidence, our amateur tennis tournament takes place in the summer, when strawberries are ripe for the picking. This inspired me to created a seasonal cake that's a play on the English Victoria sandwich, served with fresh Honey Whipped Cream and garden-grown strawberries. I look forward to sharing it with my competitors under the shade of the pavilion.

Makes one 9-inch round layer cake

Milk and Honey Cake (page 34)
Honey Whipped Cream (page 75)

1 pound (450g) strawberries, larger berries halved or quartered
Confectioners' sugar, for dusting

Preheat the oven to 350°F. Prepare pans. (Make sure to line bottom and sides with parchment.) Make the batter for the Milk and Honey Cake according to directions. Bake the cakes side by side on the same oven rack for 30 to 35 minutes or until a wooden skewer inserted in the center comes out clean, and the cake bounces back when lightly pressed. Cool the cakes completely on a wire rack. Make the Honey Whipped Cream. Put one of the cakes on a serving plate. Spoon the cream on top of the cake, keeping it 2 inches from the perimeter. (You'll will have extra to serve on the side.) Gently place the top layer of the cake onto the bottom layer. This will push the cream to the edges. To decorate, start with the whole strawberries and then pile on the halved and quartered pieces, facing both cut side in and out at various angles. Finally, dust your masterpiece with confectioners' sugar to bring out the shine and juices of the strawberries.

Bake-and-Buy-Back-Immediately Fund-Raiser Bundt

Don't be intimidated by this majestic Bundt. It's easy to pull off, works for many occasions, and is sure to win ribbons. One time while I was visiting my dad, my stepmother had baked two of these for a fund-raiser at my sister's school. Before I could ask why she had made two, she handed the cakes to my father with specific instructions: take them up to the school and buy one back immediately. Half an hour later, Dad returned as instructed, and we all enjoyed a slice with a cup of tea. This also works with the Versatile Coconut Cake recipe doubled (page 42).

**Makes one large Bundt cake
(10- to 15-cup)**

Double batch of Chocolate Coconut Cake (page 45)
Coconut Glaze (page 70)

Shredded coconut or cocoa power, for dusting
⅓ cup (20g) unsweetened coconut flakes, toasted

Preheat the oven to 350°F. Grease the Bundt pan generously with butter, using your fingers to get into all the grooves, then lightly dust with shredded coconut or cocoa, shaking off any excess. Make the batter for the Chocolate Coconut Cake according to directions. Bake for approximately 50 minutes or until a wooden skewer inserted into the Bundt comes out clean and bounces back when lightly pressed. Cool the bundt on a wire rack. While the cake bakes, make the Coconut Glaze. You want the glaze to be a consistency that clings to the cake. Evenly pour the glaze on top of the cake, until it starts to drip slightly down the sides of the cake. Before the glaze sets, sprinkle the toasted coconut around the top of the cake.

Sleepover Cake

I think one of life's great pleasures is a freshly baked dessert straight from the oven. When we have a gaggle of teenagers or friends here, I often bake the Chocolatey Chocolate Cake in ramekins. I'll serve them with Toblerone Ganache and/or Caramel Sauce and a scoop of vanilla ice cream for a lazy-ish molten cake. You can prepare both the cake batter and the ganache or sauce ahead of time. Pop the cakes in the oven while you're having dinner, so they're lovely and warm. If you don't own ramekins, a nonstick cupcake pan greased well will work.

Makes 10 to 12 ramekins

Chocolatey Chocolate Cake
(page 22)
Toblerone Ganache (page 80)
and/or **Caramel Sauce** (page 92)

Preheat the oven to 350°F. Using your fingers, grease the ramekins with butter and place them on a large, flat baking pan. Make the batter for the Chocolatey Chocolate Cake according to directions. Fill each ramekin halfway with batter; don't overfill, since this cake rises and you want to leave plenty of room for the toppings. Bake for 20 to 25 minutes or until a wooden skewer inserted in the center comes out clean, and the cake bounces back when lightly pressed. Cool slightly. While the cake bakes, make the Toblerone Ganache and/or Caramel Sauce. Place ramekins on a serving plate, take the toppings to the table and let everyone help themselves—and don't forget the ice cream.

Holiday Hazelnut Cake

I love the long lead up from Thanksgiving to the New Year—so many parties and good excuses to eat and drink too much. If you're having friends over, this is a great cake to make for dessert. The Hazelnut Gató is sophisticated and the Nutella Whipped Cream makes everyone feel right at home. Sprinkle some roughly chopped, toasted hazelnuts over each slice and let the bubbly flow. Oh, and it can all be made ahead of the party!

Makes one 9-inch round cake

Hazelnut Gató (page 57)
Nutella Whipped Cream (page 75)

¾ cup (100g) whole hazelnuts

Preheat the oven to 350°F. Prepare pan. Make the batter for the Hazelnut Gató according to directions. Bake for 30 to 35 minutes or until a wooden skewer inserted in the center comes out clean, and the cake bounces back when lightly pressed. Cool the cake on a wire rack. Meanwhile, toast the hazelnuts in the oven or in a heavy frying pan, until aromatic and lightly colored. Remove some of the blistered skins by rubbing the warm nuts vigorously in a clean dishcloth and then roughly chop. Make the Nutella Whipped Cream. To decorate, either top the entire cake with the whipped cream and sprinkle on the nuts, or alternatively, slice up the cake into individual portions, serving each slice with a dollop of cream and a sprinkling of nuts.

Vacation Cakes

It's a luxury to step outside your everyday routine and see other ways of doing things—to learn, be inspired, stop old records playing in your head, and reboot. I have vivid memories of experiencing culture shock for the first time when I was four, and my parents took my brother and me on our first overseas trip to Bali. We traveled around the island, where we slept in thatched huts, wore sarongs, and ate frogs' legs. I remember sitting on my straw bed feeling desperately homesick, daydreaming of the smell of our local butcher shop, and popsicles from the store.

When our kids were really young, my husband and I put travel on hold after a few hellish flights from New York to Sydney. In recent years, we've started traveling again. The following cakes have been inspired by travel and are often baked on vacation when I have the time to get creative and experiment. Using local produce or the complete lack of ingredients can make you a resourceful and inventive baker. Seasons and tradition spark different cravings. In summer, I want a cake that's light and tangy; in the winter, I'm looking for warmth and spice. Baking cakes discovered on your travels is an excellent way to keep the memories of the trip alive. And no, I don't think it's crazy packing a cake tin.

Mallorca

Our good friends Tom and Melissa needed a sea change. They quit their corporate jobs, packed up their Brooklyn lives, and traveled the world. They ended up resettling in Mallorca, Spain. Scratch their eyes out.

Mallorca is a Mediterranean island paradise, with an economy reliant on tourism; the tennis champion Rafael Nadal; and the farming of olives, salt, and almonds. A couple of times, my family has bravely offered to look after the kids so my husband, Nick, and I can escape to Mallorca and pretend we're Tom and Melissa. We get to eat late, sleep in, swim, and recharge. We're taken to secluded beaches, churches on mountaintops, and to hidden boutiques that we never would have discovered on our own.

One afternoon, we called into a local bakery where I had my first slice of *gató d'ametlla*. This native Mallorcan cake was so delicious I boldly went and asked the owner for the recipe. I didn't get it; instead, I got a life lesson. "It's a process, not a recipe," he said. How brilliant! When I returned home, I began my own gató journey.

(24)

Mediterranean Almond Gató

Makes one 9-inch round cake

· ·

Almond Gató (page 54)
Vanilla Whipped Cream (page 75)

¾ cup (65g) flaked almonds, toasted
Confectioners' sugar, for dusting

This summery cake is glorious served with vanilla whipped cream or vanilla gelato. If apricots are in season, grill and serve on the side.

· ·

Preheat the oven to 350°F. Prepare pan. Make the batter for the Almond Gató according to directions. Bake for 30 to 35 minutes, or until a wooden skewer inserted in the center comes out clean, and the cake bounces back when lightly pressed. Cool the cake on a wire rack.

When the cake is completely cool, sprinkle the almonds over the top of the cake and dust with confectioners' sugar. Make the Vanilla Whipped Cream. Serve alongside the cake.

Fire Island

For an Australian, summer feels short in the Northern Hemisphere. When it comes, I cherish every second. Over the last ten years we've vacationed on Fire Island, a charming barrier island not far from New York City. It's the closest experience to Australia that I can find in New York. There's nothing to do except sleep, plan menus, grill, eat, drink, swim, and be with friends. Unlike in Brooklyn, the kids are free to roam and bike without worrying about cars. At the end of the day, outdoor showers wash off the salt, sand, and the occasional bloodied big toe. We welcome the night with an icy-cold gin and tonic, an hour affectionately known as G & T o'clock.

Nick, Dixie, and Opal all have summer birthdays, so it's a tradition that I bake cakes out on Fire Island. Turning on the oven to bake during the warmer months can be a tough sell, but after a day at the beach, a home-baked treat is just the thing.

Beach Bake-Sale Madeleines

My entrepreneurial daughter and her friends always want to have bake sales. When we vacation on Fire Island, the kids make a few dollars from these sales and then go and spend up big at the ice cream store. Although I usually have to supervise and help them get the cakes in and out of the oven, I applaud their initiative. I'll miss seeing them pull their wagon full of decorated shells and baked goods to entice the beachgoers once they've outgrown this special time in their lives. Through experience, we have learned that icing in the heat isn't such a hit, so these unadorned madeleines with their nautical shells are a fitting solution.

Makes approximately 20 madeleines

Madeleines (page 50)

Confectioners' sugar, for dusting

Preheat the oven to 350°F. Prepare the madeleine pans. (Place the pans in the freezer for at least 10 minutes if you want a hump.) Make the batter for the madeleines according to directions. Bake for 8 to 10 minutes or until the edges have pulled away slightly from the shell and are golden. Cool madeleines on a wire rack. Dust with confectioners' sugar using a sifter or fine tea strainer.

Summertime S'mores Cakes

How can you go wrong with soft, gooey toasted marshmallows, chocolate, and a bit of crunch? These little cakes are my reimagining of this North American campfire classic that always ends with sticky fingers being licked. I usually make the chocolate cake in the morning, since I've found that it cuts better when it's had time to compose itself. This recipe can easily be doubled. Bake in a 15 by 11-inch sheet pan to make approximately 20 s'mores.

Makes approximately 12 s'mores cakes, cut from a 12 by 8-inch cake

Chocolatey Chocolate Cake (page 22)
Silky Marshmallow Icing (page 87)

4 (60g) graham crackers
3 tablespoons unsalted butter
2-inch round cookie cutter

Preheat the oven to 350°F. Prepare pan. Make the batter for the Chocolatey Chocolate Cake according to directions. Bake for 25 to 30 minutes or until a wooden skewer inserted in the center comes out clean, and the cake bounces back when lightly pressed. Cool the cake on wire rack.

Crush the graham crackers finely in a blender or in a ziplock bag, using a rolling pin or something heavy. In a small skillet over medium heat, melt the butter and toast the crackers until fragrant. Cool completely.

Make the Silky Marshmallow Icing just before assembling.

To assemble the s'mores: use a 2-inch round cookie cutter to punch holes out of the cake. You should get approximately 12 small round cakes if you cut them closely together. Using a sharp knife, cut the round cakes in half horizontally, keeping the knife parallel to the work surface. Place a spoonful of Silky Marshmallow Icing on one half, then place the other half on top, sandwiching the pieces together. Spoon another small dollop of the icing on top of each s'more and use the back of a spoon to get a nice lift in the icing by flicking your wrist. After all the cakes are done, sprinkle a smattering of toasted graham cracker crumbs on top. If you're lucky enough to own a cooking torch, toast the icing or put the s'mores under the broiler, being very, very careful not to burn them! (Put them in the fridge before toasting to help the icing set a little before applying heat.) Either way, they're delicious.

27

Big Daddy's Pavlova

Here's my dirty secret: I'm writing a cake book, and my husband is the one family member who isn't a big fan of cake. That should be grounds for divorce, but being the good wife, I compromise. For his birthday, I always bake him one of his favorites: an Antipodean classic, the Pavlova. This is also a great gluten-free option. The meringue works marvelously topped with Vanilla Whipped Cream and a mix of summertime fruits and berries. If you have a local farmers' market nearby, drop in and pick up a variety of what looks seasonally delicious. I like to keep the characteristics you find on farm-grown fruits, such as the small leaves on the cherries, on for decoration. Use a mix of sizes and colors of fruit in similar hues. If you can get your hands on passion fruit, it's the bomb with mango slices. I often bake the meringue in the morning and let it sit in the oven to keep it in a dry, controlled temperature until it's time to serve. Add the whipped cream and fruit just before serving, so the meringue doesn't get soft.

Makes 1 large Pavlova

Meringue (page 58)
Vanilla Whipped Cream (page 75)

3 to 4 cups of various summer berries

Preheat the oven to 300°F. Make the large meringue according to directions. Turn the oven temperature to 250°F. Bake for approximately 1 hour and 20 minutes or until the outside is crisp and the center soft. Turn off the oven and leave the meringue in the oven to cool completely.

Just before serving, make the Vanilla Whipped Cream. Spoon the cream onto the top of the meringue, leaving half an inch around the perimeter. Top with the berries: start with the larger strawberries and then pile the more-delicate berries on top.

Canada

My brother and his family live in British Columbia in a remote, secluded, sleepy town, where bears make unannounced visits, ziplines keep cousins entertained for hours, and berries grow in abundance over the summer. In early July when we visit, the sun-warmed berries look so pretty, polka-dotted against the dramatic West Coast landscape. Blueberries, raspberries, huckleberries, salmonberries, and cherries all grow wild in their backyard and are perfect for popping in cakes.

Oh, Canada! Lemon Berry Crumble Cake

Makes one 10-inch round cake

. . . .

**Lovely Lemon Yogurt Cake
(page 46)**
Berry Crumble (page 77)

Serving this cake slightly warm, with a scoop of vanilla or walnut ice cream that slowly melts into the buttery, berry crunch of the crumble, is a moment worth working toward.

. . . .

Preheat the oven to 350°F. Prepare a 10-inch spring form pan, making sure it's lined with parchment on the bottom and sides. Make the batter for the Lovely Lemon Yogurt Cake according to directions.

Make the Berry Crumble.

Fill the pan with batter and then evenly sprinkle the crumble over the top of the batter. Bake for 50 to 55 minutes until a wooden skewer inserted in the center comes out clean, and the cake bounces back when lightly pressed. Let the cake sit for 10 minutes before releasing the springform, carefully peel off the parchment paper, slice, and serve.

Upstate New York

The first time we drove to upstate New York, I was surprised to see how quickly the congested city turns into vast rural areas. City dwellers escape there for weekends, to ski in the winter, swim and hike in the summer, and to pick seasonal harvests in the fall. The kids love our annual pilgrimage to pick apples and bring home pumpkins to carve. We go to a pick-your-own apple orchard and fill bags with Empires, Galas, Fujis, Honeycrisps, McIntosh, and Golden Delicious. If you go early in the morning, the apples on the trees are cool and crisp, and the fallen ones create obstacles and weapons for the kids to throw at each other. We always have an excess that I need to get creative with, so I often make the following cakes to use them up. I prefer to bake with apples that are tart and crisp since they balance out a cake's sweetness and tend to hold their shape better.

Diced Cinnamon Donut Cakes

If you have an apple-cider-donut craving, this is the cake to bake. I've always been a sucker for a hot donut covered in cinnamon sugar. At the farm stands in upstate New York, you'll often find them. One whiff and you're ordering a lazy dozen. As a teenager, I used to ask for a donut cake, so my mother would go out, buy a dozen donuts, stack them on top of each other, and put candles on top. Inspired by this memory, one year for one of Opal's larger birthdays I doubled the recipe for the Cinnamon Spice Cake and baked it in a sheet pan. Then I cut it into small squares, brushed some melted butter over each piece, and sprinkled each with cinnamon sugar. For the presentation, I followed Mom's lead, piling the squares on top of each other and finishing with natural beeswax candles. These squares are a nice change from the usual buttercream birthday suspects. They look natural and simple, and the kids gobble them up. I put any leftover pieces of cake in waxed bags for the kids to take home. (Does anyone else remember when you went home from the party with a slice of cake? Or is that just an Australian thing?) These squares are also great for school birthday celebrations. You could probably cut the amount of sugar and cinnamon in half, but it's lovely to have an abundance of sugar sprinkled on the pile. For a smaller family affair, make a single batch and use a 13 by 9-inch rectangular pan. Bake for 28 to 30 minutes.

Makes one 15 by 11-inch sheet cake (approximately 55 mini squares)

Double batch Cinnamon Spice Cake (page 30)

⅔ cup (140g) cane sugar

2 teaspoons ground cinnamon

6 tablespoons (85g) unsalted butter, melted

Preheat the oven to 350°F. Prepare pan. Make the batter for the Cinnamon Spice Cake according to directions. Bake for 30 to 35 minutes or until a wooden skewer inserted in the center comes out clean, and the cake bounces back when lightly pressed. Cool the cake on a wire rack. With a large, sharp knife, cut the edges off the cake. Use a ruler as a guide if you want the cake cut into perfect cubes; if not, do it by eye.

Mix the sugar and cinnamon in a small bowl.

Brush or spoon the melted butter on top of each cake square. Let it soak into the cake a little before sprinkling on the cinnamon-sugar mix. (If the cake is still warm, the sugar will dissolve.) Stack the squares on top of each other into a pyramid and serve.

Fall Apple Skillet Cake

Here's a dessert that's perfect for a large fall dinner party, like ones we have at our friend's house upstate. Bring the two rustic skillets straight from the oven to the table to serve up. This cake is a cross between an apple cake and English pudding, so it is best eaten warm. Sprinkling melted butter, sugar, and cinnamon on the apples enables them to be slighty caramelized before they are enveloped by the batter. It's not like a pie or a tart, so don't hate me when the apple slices sink in. I've baked this cake in numerous ways and prefer it when the apples get all gooey and delicious from baking in the batter. Serve with Crème Anglaise, Honey Whipped Cream, or vanilla ice cream.

Makes two 9-inch round cakes

Milk and Honey Cake (page 34)
Crème Anglaise (page 91) or
Honey Whipped Cream (page 75)

4 apples, cored and thinly sliced
½ cup (120ml) freshly squeezed lemon juice
2 tablespoon unsalted butter, melted
6 tablespoons (80g) cane sugar
½ teaspoon ground cinnamon

Preheat the oven to 350°F. Grease two 9-inch cast iron skillets with butter or prepare springform pans, making sure they're lined.

In a small bowl, toss the apple slices in lemon juice to stop them from browning, cover with plastic wrap, and set aside.

Make the batter for the Milk and Honey Cake according to directions. Divide the batter evenly between the skillets or pans and smooth the tops with a spatula. Working from the center out, gently lay the apple slices on top of the batter; leave behind any excess juice. Brush or drizzle the melted butter over the apple slices. Mix the sugar and cinnamon together and sprinkle evenly over the apple slices. Bake for approximately 30 minutes or until golden. A skewer may not come out completely clean due to the moisture of the apple, but it shouldn't be wet. If baked in a springform pan, let sit for 10 minutes then release and remove parchment paper. Serve with Créme Anglaise.

TIPS: For the decorative top, reserve one-third of the apple slices, and after the cake has baked for 20 minutes, place the remaining apples on top of the cake. Work quickly, so you don't lose all the oven's hot air. This may add on a couple of minutes to the bake time. Alternatively, hasselback the apples and place in the batter. This recipe can be halved.

A Flavor Chart

In *Simple Cake*, some combinations hum more than others, and not every topping goes with every cake. This charts helps guide you toward mixing and matching cakes and toppings

TOPPINGS \ CAKES	Chocolatey Chocolate Cake	Very Vanilla Cake	Cinnamon Spice Cake	Milk and Honey Cake	Tangy Olive Oil Cake	Versatile Coconut Cake	Lovely Lemon Yogurt Cake	Madeleines	Almond Gató	Meringue
Nana's Simple Glaze		•		•	•	•	•	•		
Easy Creamy Icing		•		•	•	•	•			
Beautiful Buttercream	•	•								
White and Whipped Cream	•	•	•	•	•	•	•	•	•	•
Cream Cheese Frosting			•			•	•			
Berry Crumble		•	•			•	•			
Citrus Syrup					•	•	•	•		
Toblerone Ganache	•	•				•		•	•	
Tres Leches	•					•				
Compote	•	•	•	•		•	•	•	•	•
Raspberry Curd					•	•	•	•		•
Silky Marshmallow Icing	•						•			
Chocolate Swiss Meringue Buttercream	•	•								
Crème Anglaise	•			•	•	•		•	•	•
Caramel Sauce	•			•						•

Ingredients

When a recipe has only five or six ingredients, like many in this book, you need them to be the best you can afford. Each ingredient has a specific role in the success of a cake.

FLOUR

Flour provides structure in a cake. I like to bake with various flours, but often the cake I bake is determined by the flour I have in my pantry. Each type of flour has its own protein content, characteristics, and weight that affect the cake's flavor and crumb. A specific flour's qualities can also vary slightly from brand to brand.

If you are in the mood to experiment, some of the cake recipes in this book are robust enough to withstand an interchange of flours. The trick is to use the same weight of flour rather than volume in the substitution. See ingredient weights and measures (on back endpapers). For example, I've successfully baked the Chocolatey Chocolate Cake (page 22) using both all-purpose flour and spelt flour. The Very Vanilla Cake (page 26) works nicely with cake flour instead of all-purpose flour, and the Milk and Honey Cake (page 34) is also spectacular made with cake flour. Just be mindful that the baking times might be slightly different based on your flour selection.

All-Purpose Flour

This is your run-of-the-mill general use flour. Because it has a higher-protein content, it's a sturdy flour. I usually buy King Arthur organic, GMO-free, unbleached all-purpose flour.

Cake Flour

With its low-protein content, this soft flour gets easily absorbed into liquids and retains moisture while producing a light, delicate, fine crumb. You might like to try cake flour in the Very Vanilla Cake (page 26) or the Milk and Honey Cake (page 34). Just make sure you put the same weight of flour in the cake. If you can't get your hands on

cake flour, you can make your own similar ingredient by sifting together three parts all-purpose flour and one part cornstarch. I bake with White Lily or King Arthur flour.

Spelt Flour

Don't be intimidated by this up-and-coming ancient grain. Many bakers are discovering this gem of a flour, since it's very light and has a nutty, wholesome air about it. I buy stone-ground, whole-grain spelt. Spelt still contains gluten but absorbs liquid easily, so gluten-sensitive people often find it easier to digest. If you want a healthier, nutrient-rich flour, spelt is an excellent alternative. I've successfully substituted spelt in the Chocolatey Chocolate Cake (page 22) and the Milk and Honey Cake (page 34).

Gluten-Free Flour

Each time I walk past the flour section in a supermarket, it appears there's a new brand of gluten-free flour. I find gluten-free flour to be light and absorbent. Some years ago, when I needed to refrain from gluten, I used Thomas Keller's Cup4Cup gluten-free flour because it was the only one on the market I could buy. It's a mix of cornstarch, white rice flour, brown rice flour, milk powder, tapioca flour, potato starch, and xanthan gum. A lot of gluten-free flours are blends, because with the absence of wheat, the flour needs to get structure by combining various types of gluten-free ingredients to mimic the properties of regular flour. More recently, I've used Bob's Red Mill Gluten-Free All-Purpose Baking Flour, which is a mix of stone-ground gluten-free grain and bean flours. It has quite an earthy flavor. It can be substituted 1:1 with regular all-purpose flour. I'm not an expert in gluten-free flours, so if you have a brand you're familiar with and like, I'd start with that.

Nut Flours

Hazelnuts and almonds can be ground to create flavorsome flours that cannot be matched. You can make your own at home, but I'm lazy and buy mine. You can purchase superfine almond flour that creates a lighter, delicate cake or almond meal that produces a more rustic crumb. Both work equally well in the Gatò (page 54). Bob's Red Mill sells all of the nut types mentioned above. They're more expensive than some other flours, but the flavor is worth every penny.

Storage of Flours

Store flours in airtight containers so they don't absorb moisture or odors from the fridge. Store nut and nutrient-rich flours in the fridge or freezer in an airtight container or in a large ziplock bag to keep them fresh, since they can quickly turn rancid. Make sure you bring the flour up to room temperature before use. Aerate and break up any lumps that may have formed with a spoon.

LEAVENERS

Leaveners help aerate a cake and make it rise. The aeration adds volume and influences texture. Sift leaveners with flour to evenly distribute them throughout the batter so the cake rises uniformly. I use both natural and chemical leaveners in *Simple Cake*. Leavening is achieved by the choice of ingredient and the method of preparation.

Natural Leaveners

Butter. Beaten butter traps air bubbles that then expand in the heat of the oven. If creamed with sugar, butter is an even more successful leavener. Butter also contains water that converts to steam in the oven.

Eggs. When yolks and especially whites are beaten, air bubbles are created. These air bubbles expand in the heat of the oven, helping the cake rise.

Chemical Leaveners

Baking powder. A mixture of baking soda and cream of tartar, baking powder is often mixed with a little cornstarch to stop it from taking on moisture and to lengthen its shelf life. It is activated by liquid and heat and produces carbon dioxide. Baking powder is gluten-free. I like Rumford

Baking Powder because it's aluminum free and GMO free. Make sure you check the expiration date. It's helpful to write the date on the package when you first open it. If it's more than a year old, you may want to throw it out, as it will probably have lost its fizz, and your cake may not rise to its full potential. To check if it's still good, put ½ teaspoon in ½ cup of water and look for immediate fizz.

Baking soda. Sodium bicarbonate, commonly known as baking soda, creates carbon dioxide when combined with an acid. That's why using it with buttermilk, cocoa, honey, or citrus can create a delightful texture that can balance out its strong flavor. Use baking soda sparingly, since a little goes a long way. Store in an airtight container. To check if your baking soda is still good, put ½ teaspoon in some vinegar and watch for fizz.

Cream of tartar. A powdered form of tartaric acid, cream of tartar is used to stabilize egg whites, prevent sugar from crystallizing, make meringues whiter, and increase volume by helping these ingredients hold water and air. If you're out of vinegar, you can substitute ¼ teaspoon of cream of tartar in the Meringue recipe (page 58), since both vinegar and cream of tartar are acidic. Cream of tartar will keep indefinitely in a cool, dry spot.

SALT

The addition of salt in small quantities balances out sweetness and enhances other flavor profiles. The type, size, and density per measure of salt will affect how salty a recipe will be. I save the more expensive, larger, flaky sea salts like fleur de sel or Maldon for texture, garnish, and decoration and use the less-expensive, finer, everyday salt like Diamond Crystal Kosher Salt for the batter. Kosher salt is preferred by many cooks, since it doesn't contain iodine or anticaking agents, is easy to measure, and gets absorbed quickly. Table salt is stronger due to its finer crystals. Of course, you can use whichever fine salt you have in the pantry. Just remember, cake batter needs only a pinch of salt; you can always add more, but you won't be able to take any away.

FATS

Cakes need fat for leavening and flavor and to help keep them moist. Fat also coats the proteins in flour, inhibiting the activation of too much gluten that can dry cakes out.

Butter

Boutique American butters and many European butters have a high milk fat content and often have cultures added. These butters are perfect for baking and can add a tang to the overall flavor. I generally use standard American unsalted butter that contains no less than 80 percent milk fat, because that's what I have in the fridge, and it's easy to buy at the supermarket. Using unsalted butter helps control the amount of salt that goes into a cake. If all you have in the fridge is salted butter, think about reducing the amount of salt you add to the batter. When room temperature butter is beaten with sugar, it creates and traps air bubbles, helping your cake to rise. Butter is ready to use when you press your finger on the surface and it leaves an indentation. I never use margarine and avoid sprays when greasing my pans. For storing, securely wrap butter, since it picks up other flavors from the fridge. It can also be frozen.

Oil

Oil keeps cakes ridiculously moist. My choice of oils in *Simple Cake* are extra-virgin olive oil, grapeseed oil, and extra-virgin coconut oil. I use these oils for their appropriateness in the overall flavor of the cake. For the Tangy Olive Oil Cake (page 38), I prefer to use a delicate, buttery olive oil. If you think your olive oil seems too herbaceous or pungent, trust your instincts and try something milder. My sister-in-law put me onto grapeseed oil, a nice, light neutral oil that works great in the Chocolatey Chocolate Cake (page 22) and the Lovely Lemon Yogurt Cake (page 46). (Canola oil is a substitute if you don't have grapeseed oil.)

EGGS

Eggs help bind a cake, and they add fat, liquid, and flavor. I use organic free-range eggs. One afternoon, I was baking with my friend Simon, who was visiting from Ireland, and he commented on how the eggs we were using seemed smaller than the ones he uses in the United Kingdom. Standard egg sizes vary across countries. I developed the recipes in this book using large eggs that weigh approximately 2 ounces in the shell. Eggs should be at room temperature before baking. If you've forgotten to take the eggs out of the fridge, expedite the process by putting them in a bowl of warm water for five minutes and pat them dry before cracking them.

DAIRY

Dairy adds flavor, moisture, and fat to a cake.

Milk

Whole milk adds both fat and liquid to a cake, thereby adding flavor and moisture. Forget skim milk; it's dead to you.

Heavy Cream or Heavy Whipping Cream

These creams have a high percentage of fat and therefore have more flavor. The fat content also enables them to be whipped more easily when chilled, creating voluminous, pillowy peaks.

Buttermilk

Buttermilk adds a mild, tangy flavor to cakes while also adding moisture and tenderness to the final product. The acidity of buttermilk breaks down the gluten and activates the leaveners to create carbon dioxide, making for an airier cake. Shake the bottle well before using. If you don't have buttermilk on hand and you're in a pinch, make your own by souring milk: add 1 tablespoon of lemon juice or white vinegar to 1 cup of whole milk. Let it sit for five to ten minutes or until it looks curdled. You can freeze excess buttermilk for another time, or better still, use it to make fried chicken for dinner.

Mascarpone

Mascarpone is a rich, creamy Italian cheese that's high in butterfat and adds a creamy tang to sweet recipes.

SWEETENERS

Structurally, these cake recipes need sugar to succeed. The sugar sweetens, helps create air bubbles when you beat it into butter, tenderizes the cake by softening the proteins in the flour, gives the cake its golden color, and keeps the cake moist after baking. Sugar, like salt, enhances other flavors; however, processed, refined sugar is not feeling the love right now. It's recently been on trial, and the verdict isn't looking good. I've been mindful of the sugar content in these recipes and have tried to reduce it without compromising the taste and structural integrity. I believe if you have a slice of homemade cake, you don't need to beat yourself up. Unlike store-bought cakes or other snack foods that have additives and preservatives, you will know exactly what has gone into your cake and how much sugar you've consumed.

Granulated Sugar and Caster Sugar (Superfine)

Fine-textured cane sugars are perfect for creating cakes with a delicate crumb. Both granulated and caster sugar are great for creaming with butter. Caster sugar is preferable for dissolving in egg whites to make Meringue (page 58), since it's finer than granulated sugar. If I don't have caster sugar on hand, I make my own by grinding granulated sugar in a food processor or with a mortar and pestle. Just watch that you don't turn it into powdered sugar. Alternatively, if you're desperate, you can put granulated sugar in a ziplock bag and bang it out with a rolling pin.

Unrefined Cane Sugar

This type of cane sugar has a golden color and larger sugar granules that can add a welcome crunch when sprinkled on a fall cake like the Cinnamon Spice Cake (page 30).

Confectioners' Sugar

This is powdered cane sugar with the addition of cornstarch. A very fine powdered sugar that dissolves easily, it's perfect for dusting your cakes or for making toppings like the Easy Creamy Icing (page 72) or the Beautiful Buttercream (page 73). Dust the cake as close to serving time as possible, as the sugar will be absorbed into the cake over time.

Brown Sugar

Brown sugar brings a sweet warmth and depth of flavor to a cake. It's available in light or dark brown, depending on how much molasses has been added. Lightly pack your measuring cups. Store in an airtight container, since it can get lumpy and dry out easily.

Honey

This natural sweetener adds liquid and a delicate sweetness to cakes. There are different grades of honey, based on moisture content, absences of defects, flavor, aroma and color. It's preferable to use a Grade A honey, or quality honey from a local beekeeper at the farmers' market or specialty supermarkets. Use a runny honey, since it's easier to measure. Cakes will have a darker exterior when baked with honey, so make sure you line the baking pan with parchment paper to stop your cake from sticking and taking on too much color.

Golden Syrup

Similar to honey, golden syrup gives a lovely warmth and sweetness to baked goods. It's a sugar cane syrup. It's very popular in Australia and in the United Kingdom, but it's not as common here in the United States. Look for it in the baking aisle at specialty supermarkets like Whole Foods Market. I use Lyle's Golden Syrup.

FLAVORINGS

Once the foundation of your cake has been built, you are free to play with flavor. Choose whatever flavor suits your cravings or the occasion. Here are a few of my favorites.

Vanilla

Vanilla awakens other flavors in a recipe and cannot be rivaled. It's baking royalty, the queen of cakes. Be sure to choose pure vanilla extract, not imitation flavor or essence. Add the extract last to warm toppings like Crème Anglaise (page 91) or Compote (page 83), so the liquor in the vanilla doesn't burn off and lose all of its flavor. I use vanilla bean seeds for special occasions, such as when I'm making the Very Vanilla Cake (page 26) or the Crème Anglaise (page 91). I buy Nielsen-Massey extract and beans and Madécasse, a great Brooklyn brand.

Chocolate

Chocolate adds a luxurious depth of flavor that satisfies cravings like no other flavor. If vanilla is the queen, chocolate is the king. Knowing the type of chocolate and the percentage of cocoa solids it contains allows you to control the intensity and sweetness in baked goods. I'm not a purist when it comes to chocolate. My kids and I are not huge fans of the bitterness of dark chocolate, so my preference for toppings is to use semisweet chocolate with its hint of vanilla. If you prefer the darker kind, you can easily substitute dark or bittersweet chocolate for semisweet in the Chocolate Sour Cream Ganache Frosting (page 80). I use good chocolate like Guittard or Ghirardelli in the form of chocolate chips, since they melt more evenly. Occasionally, I will sprinkle a handful of chocolate chips on top of a batter to save having to ice a cake or cupcakes. For decorating cakes, I buy a block of chocolate and use my vegetable peeler to create shavings.

Cocoa Powder (Dutch Processed)

Cakes made with cocoa powder will differ in flavor and texture from cakes made with chocolate. In *Simple Cake*, I use cocoa powder in the batter and save chocolate for the toppings. In particular, I use unsweetened Dutch-processed cocoa powder that has a smoother flavor and adds a lovely depth of color. Dutch-processed cocoa powder is less acidic than regular cocoa powder. In the Chocolatey Chocolate Cake (page 22), I pair unsweetened Dutch-processed cocoa powder, which has had the cocoa butter removed, with oil to create a supermoist texture, even when the cake is chilled. Droste Cacao is my go-to brand.

Fruit

Cake loves fruit. The acidity of fruit complements and cuts through sweetness and adds fragrance and tang. Some batters and toppings in *Simple Cake* call for the addition of fruit in a range of different forms, including whole, sliced, pureed, juiced, and zested. If a fruit, especially berries, is out of season, use frozen ones to bake in the batter or make Compote (page 83) or Berry Crumble (page 77). Be mindful that the water content of fruit is a factor in the moisture content of a cake if riffing on the amount of fruit you add.

Seasonal fruit can also be served on the side of a slice of cake or piled on top of Meringue (page 58). It will add an instant pop of color and looks pretty on the plate as well. Think about grilling stone fruits with infused sugars in the summer or poaching pears and apples with spices in the fall to accompany your cake.

Nuts

Because of their natural oils, nuts bring moisture and so much flavor and texture to a cake. Nuts can be incorporated whole, chopped, slivered, or ground into the batter or simply sprinkled on top. You can't beat the contrast of a little crunch in (or on top of) a soft cake. Almonds, hazelnuts, pistachios, walnuts, and pecans all work with cake. Lightly toast nuts to really bring out their flavors. Nuts do have a limited shelf life, so before using, make sure they haven't turned rancid. If you are folding chopped nuts into a batter, lightly dust the nuts in flour first to stop them from sinking to the bottom of the cake.

Spices

Spices enhance a cake's flavor profile. They are aromatic and can be mellow, warm, nutty, or sweet, depending on the type used. Ground cinnamon, nutmeg, allspice, cardamom, poppy seed, and ginger are great spices for cakes. Sift ground spices with the dry ingredients to incorporate them evenly. You might like to try ¼ to ½ teaspoon of ground cardamom in the Versatile Coconut Cake (page 42), for example, or 1½ teaspoons of ground ginger in the Milk and Honey Cake (page 34). Remember, spices have an expiration date and should be kept in airtight containers. That said, I have been guilty when desperate of reaching in the pantry and using a spice that looks suspiciously old.

Herbs and Edible Flowers

Infusing the flavor of herbs and edible flowers into a cake or topping can add intriguing aromatics and flare to the simplest of cakes. As you become familiar with these classic recipes, you may enjoy experimenting and playing around by infusing flavors. Be mindful that you don't want to overpower the cake, so err on the side of less is more. Start in the garden to find inspiration, because there's nothing more therapeutic than pottering round the garden picking herbs and blooms to bake into a cake or to use for decoration. Or the next time you're at the farmers' market, pick up a few small potted herbs to keep in the kitchen. Basil, edible lavender, mint, rosemary, rose petals, sage, and thyme are easy-to-get-your-hands-on flavors.

Infused Sugars

To infuse sugar, use your fingers, a mortar and pestle, or a spice grinder to crush and work leafy and flowering herbs, citrus zest, or vanilla bean seeds into the sugar. If you don't want any added texture, make sure you use a grinder or run sugar through a sieve before using. Alternatively, place some sugar and an ingredient like a used vanilla bean in a clean, dry, sealed jar for a couple of weeks to infuse the flavor into the sugar. (These can make wonderful gifts.)

Just make sure the added flavoring is dry to prevent the sugar from clumping. Infused sugars may also be sprinkled on top of a cake.

Infused Syrups and Glazes

To infuse syrups or glazes simply steep herbs, edible flowers, citrus zest, or spices in the liquid used to make a syrup or glaze. Like tea, if the liquid is warm, it will help draw out the flavor. Strain the infused liquid before using unless the leaves are very delicate and pretty like thyme. Alternatively, rose and orange waters add distinct perfume and taste to a syrup or glaze.

About the Author

Odette Williams is an Australian who now calls Brooklyn home. She is an avid home baker and cake eater. She is also the founder of OW Brooklyn, a brand that believes slowing down and cooking and eating with loved ones is one of life's simple pleasures worth investing in.

Over the years, she has experienced firsthand the highs and lows of cake baking like . . .

The year her dad ambitiously tried to pull off making the coveted "pool cake" from *The Australian Women's Weekly Children's Birthday Cake Book*. It was a round butter cake with green Jell-O on top and a perimeter of store-bought chocolate biscuits that contained the Jell-O. Sounds simple enough, right? Not so much. She woke in the middle of the night to hear her dad swearing like a trooper because the chocolate biscuits had not held up their end of the bargain, leaking Jell-O throughout the fridge. She can see him now, tired from staying up late baking, stressed from work and from juggling old and new wives, yet wanting to be a great dad. There he was, cigarette in mouth, on all fours, cleaning up the green slime in the days before there were paper towels.

Or the time the paper awning that framed her birthday cake caught fire, creating a cake inferno.

Or the occasion when she made her stepdaughter Dixie a cake shaped like a duck, and its head slid off as they all sang "Happy Birthday."

Or the year when one of the kids was on a restricted diet, and she attempted to make a vegan cake that turned out like a bad crepe.

Or the night that she and a friend stayed up late making flags for a World Cup themed cake, taking far too many liberties with the flag designs.

Or the day she put too much baking soda in a cake, causing it to rise to dizzying heights and then collapsing in a crater.

Or the time her friends made a cake inspired by Mariah Carey and James Packer's unlikely romantic interlude on a boat on the French Riviera. Let's just say there were two voluptuous mounds of cake, and it was messy.

Acknowledgments

It takes a village to write a cookbook. Here's mine.

Mikaela Martin, thank you for listening, brainstorming, laughing, having a deep understanding of my vision, and helping me bring this book to life. You wore many hats and brought your heart, empathy, and creativity to the project. Tony would be proud. I would do it again in a heartbeat. Nicole Franzen, your eye, talent, and heart have captured the spirit of this book beautifully. You always come with your sleeves rolled up, ready to raise the bar, and go above and beyond to make the best work possible. Suzie Myers, for seamlessly stepping in to help with props in the second inning. (Thanks, Jan.)

To my Ten Speed team, who have championed *Simple Cake* from day one. Hannah, Emma, Mari, Jane, Kristin, Aly, Windy, and Allison, I feel so privileged to work with such talented, kind women. Kelly Snowden, you have been the dream editor. Thank you for understanding what it's like to have cake batter run through your veins. My wonderful agent, Kari Stuart, at ICM for the hug after our first meeting and continued support and belief since.

Anne White, for pressing play on *Simple Cake*. Marisa Dobson, for delivering the proposal pitch-perfect. Amy Chaplin, for mentoring me through the cookbook process. Brett Stiller, for your weekend baking, belly laughs, companionship, and support at all the crucial times.

Simon D'Arcy, for always being an inspiration in the kitchen and helping me narrow down, test, and refine the recipe selection. Joanna Keohane, for recipe testing so thoughtfully. Caren Tommasone, for your baking wisdom and flair on the second shoot. Mimi Demas, my talented intern, for turning up on day one with a baked cake.

Amy, Sean, Julia, Luke, and Jack Lyons, for being our Brooklyn family. Mark, Deb, and Isabelle D'Arcy, our other New York family. Thank you for having the door always open for our family and *Simple Cake*! May we have many more meals and memories together.

Thomas Bossert and Melissa Rosenbauer, for the Espanyolet linens. Marissa Buick of Soor Ploom. Ingrid Carozzi and Tin Can Studio. Vikram and Meeru Vij, Hillary Bell, Susan Shapiro, and Emma Magenta.

To Mum, for making February and a few other months all about cake and being my biggest cheerleader and greatest role model. Jenny Williams, for loving dad and teaching me so much about baking. Charlene Conlin, Deborah Lloyd, and Claudia Lloyd Hensley. Matt Schneider, Rachel Geisler, Mira Gilchrist, Leslie Koren, Kazuho and Mei Ozawa, Tone Voke, Anita Menyangbo. To Dixie, Matilda, Opal, and Ned, who graciously shared me with cake for more than a year. And finally, to Nick: this is all for you.

Index

Published in the United States by Ten Speed Press, an imprint of the
Crown Publishing Group, a division of Penguin Random House LLC, New York.
www.crownpublishing.com
www.tenspeed.com

Ten Speed Press and the Ten Speed Press colophon are registered
trademarks of Penguin Random House LLC.

Library of Congress Cataloging-in-Publication Data
    Names: Williams, Odette, author. | Franzen, Nicole, photographer.
    Title: Simple cake : all you need to keep your friends and family in cake /
        by Odette Williams ; photography by Nicole Franzen.
    Description: California : Ten Speed Press, [2019] | Includes bibliographical
        references and index.
    Identifiers: LCCN 2018025094 | ISBN 9780399581427 (hardcover)
    Subjects: LCSH: Cake. | LCGFT: Cookbooks.
    Classification: LCC TX771 .W457 2019 | DDC 641.86/53—dc23
    LC record available at https://lccn.loc.gov/2018025094

Hardcover ISBN: 978-0-399-58142-7
eBook ISBN: 978-0-399-58143-4

Printed in China

Design by Emma Campion
Food styling by Odette Williams and Mikaela Martin
Prop styling by Odette Williams, Suzie Myers, and Mikaela Martin

10 9 8 7 6 5 4 3 2 1

First Edition

Ingredient Weights & Measures

Units of measurement vary around the world. The United States uses the imperial system of measurement, while Canada, the United Kingdom, and Australia use the metric system. I've included the conversions below as a guide. The equivalents are approximate; I rounded some amounts for ease of measuring.

CHOCOLATE

1 cup semisweet chocolate chips = 170g, 6 ounces

1 cup shaved chocolate = 115g, 4 ounces

1 cup Dutch-processed cocoa powder = 85g, 3 ounces

CITRUS (approximate weights since sizes vary)

1 lemon = 2 teaspoons finely grated zest = 3 tablespoons juice

1 lime = 1½ teaspoons finely grated zest = 2 tablespoons juice

1 orange = 1 tablespoon finely grated zest = ⅓ cup juice

DAIRY

1 cup whole milk = 240ml, 8 fluid ounces

1 cup buttermilk = 240ml, 8 fluid ounces

1 cup Greek yogurt = 230g, 8 ounces

1 cup sour cream = 230g, 8 ounces

1 cup heavy cream = 240ml, 8 fluid ounces

1 cup cream cheese = 225g, 8 ounces

1 cup mascarpone = 230g, 8 ounces

1 14-ounce can sweetened condensed milk = 397g

1 12-ounce can evaporated milk = 354ml

EGGS (approximate weights since eggs vary in size)

Large egg in shell = 56g, 2 ounces

Large egg out of shell = 50g, 1.75 ounces

Large egg yolk = 20g, 0.65 ounces

Large egg white = 30g, 1 ounce

FATS

1 cup butter = 16 tablespoons, 225g, 8 ounces

1 cup extra-virgin olive oil = 240ml, 8 fluid ounces

1 cup grapeseed oil = 240ml, 8 fluid ounces

1 cup extra-virgin coconut oil = 240ml, 8 fluid ounces

FLOUR

1 cup all-purpose flour, unbleached = 130g, 4.5 ounces

1 cup cake flour, unbleached = 120g, 4.0 ounces

1 cup gluten-free, all-purpose flour = 130g, 4.5 ounces

1 cup hazelnut flour = 90g, 3 ounces

1 cup almond flour = 90g, 3 ounces

1 cup whole spelt flour = 120g, 4 ounces

NUTS

½ cup pecans = 55g, 2 ounces

½ cup walnuts = 55g, 2 ounces

½ cup hazelnuts = 65g, 2 ounces

½ cup flaked almonds = 55g, 2 ounces

SALTS & LEAVENERS

1 teaspoon kosher salt = 3g

1 teaspoon sea salt = 5g

1 teaspoon baking powder = 5g

1 teaspoon baking soda = 5g

SUGAR AND SWEETENERS

1 cup granulated sugar = 200g, 7 ounces

1 cup confectioners' sugar = 115g, 4 ounces

1 cup cane sugar = 215g, 7.5 ounces

1 cup lightly packed brown sugar = 190g, 6.5 ounces

½ cup honey = 170g, 170ml, 6 ounces

½ cup maple syrup = 150g, 150ml, 5 ounces

INGREDIENT EQUIVALENTS

All-purpose flour = plain flour

Baking soda = bicarbonate of soda

Confectioners' sugar = icing sugar

Ground nut flours like almond or hazelnut can often be labeled as meal.

Conversions

VOLUME

1 teaspoon = 5ml

1 tablespoon = 15ml, 3 teaspoons

¼ cup (2 fluid ounces) = 60ml, 4 tablespoons

½ cup (4 fluid ounces) = 120ml, 8 tablespoons

¾ cup (6 fluid ounces) = 180ml, 12 tablespoons

1 cup (8 fluid ounces) = 240ml, 16 tablespoons

LENGTH

1 inch = 2.5cm

2 inches = 5cm

3 inches = 8cm

5 inches = 13cm

7 inches = 18cm

8 inches = 20cm

9 inches = 23cm

10 inches = 25cm

12 inches = 30cm

TEMPERATURE

225 °F = 110 °C

250 °F = 120 °C

275 °F = 135 °C

300 °F = 150 °C

325 °F = 165 °C

350 °F = 175 °C

375 °F = 190 °C

400 °F = 205 °C

425 °F = 220 °C

450 °F = 230 °C

475 °F = 245 °C

500 °F = 260 °C